Trauma and Disability in Mad Max

Mick Broderick • Katie Ellis

Trauma and Disability in Mad Max

Beyond the Road Warrior's Fury

palgrave
macmillan

Mick Broderick
School of Arts
Murdoch University
Murdoch, WA, Australia

Katie Ellis
School of Media, Creative Arts and Social Inquiry
Curtin University of Technology
Perth, WA, Australia

ISBN 978-3-030-19438-3 ISBN 978-3-030-19439-0 (eBook)
https://doi.org/10.1007/978-3-030-19439-0

This Palgrave Pivot imprint is published by the registered company Springer Nature Switzerland AG
The registered company address is: Gewerbestrasse 11, 6330 Cham, Switzerland

To the cinematic road warriors
past, present and future

Acknowledgements

We have incurred many debts in the researching and writing of this book, especially to our creative and generous colleagues in the vibrant fields of critical trauma and critical disability studies. We hope this book will continue the conversations already taking place within and across these disciplines.

At Palgrave, we thank Shaun Vigil for his immediate support for the concept of this book and his incisive comments and Camille Davies for taking the book to press. We also wish to thank the anonymous reviewers of the manuscript for their thoughtful comments, to which we hope we have done justice.

Throughout the period of researching and writing this book, we have had the privilege of working with two excellent research assistants—Theresa Miller and Rosemary Stevens. We also thank Ceridwen Clocherty for her work in preparing the final manuscript.

Some key aspects of Chap. 5 first appeared in Mick's essay "Heroic Apocalypse: Mad Max, Mythology and the Millennium" in Christopher Sharrett's 1993 edited collection *Crisis Cinema: The Apocalyptic Idea in Postmodern Film* (Washington, DC: Maisonneuve Press). Mick would like to thank Ross Gibson for his invaluable and insightful "yondering" across the *Mad Max* cultural terrain during his PhD candidature more than two decades ago. Mick thanks Katie Ellis for her diligence and scholarly acumen and for being such a tolerant (and fun) co-author. Mick also thanks Christine Spiegel for her support, wisdom and grace throughout the research and writing.

Katie would like to thank Curtin University and her colleagues in the discipline of Internet Studies, especially Leanne McRae and Gwyneth Peaty, for their support and willingness to discuss *Mad Max*. She is also grateful to the Australian Research Council for the privilege of her Discovery Early Career Researcher Award (DE 130101712), of which this book is an output. Katie would like to thank Mick Broderick for a great partnership in collaborating on this book, his suggestion to go see *Fury Road* immediately and for his encyclopaedic knowledge of *Mad Max*. Finally, Katie thanks Chris, Stella and Connor Pearce for their love, patience and support but mostly for putting up with her watching the *Mad Max* movies on repeat "for work".

Contents

List of Figures

CHAPTER 1

Introduction

Abstract To open the book, we introduce critical trauma studies and critical disability studies to argue that it is time these two theoretical approaches entered into a productive conversation. The Mad Max series of films traversing a period of almost 40 years is the ideal text to prompt such a discussion. The character Max Rockatansky transitioned from able-bodied masculinity in the first film to a limping, maddened road warrior in *The Road Warrior* and, by *Fury Road*, to a man haunted by guilt and hallucinations, often presenting as post-traumatic stress disorder (PTSD) but rediscovering himself and his humanity. The origins and intentions of both critical trauma and critical disability studies are outlined to examine the sites of divergence and intersection. Focusing on a humanities approach to both trauma and disability, this chapter highlights productive areas of intersection related to aesthetics, metaphor, embodiment and social-cultural critique.

Keywords Mad Max • Critical trauma studies • Critical disability studies • Aesthetics • Embodiment

The dystopian Australian action film franchise *Mad Max* traverses the period from the late-1970s to mid-2010s, beginning with *Mad Max* (1979) and producing three sequels—*Mad Max 2,* aka *The Road Warrior* (1981), *Mad Max: Beyond Thunderdome* (1985) and, most recently, *Mad*

M. Broderick, K. Ellis, *Trauma and Disability in Mad Max*,
https://doi.org/10.1007/978-3-030-19439-0_1

Max: Fury Road (2015). The entire series is well known for deploying narratives and imagery of trauma, both physical and emotional. The series creator, writer-director-producer Dr George Miller has often described his initial impetus for crafting a work set in a dystopian future as one based on his clinical experiences as an Emergency Room physician dealing with the horrendous road carnage he would regularly confront during his hospital shifts (Mathews, 1984; Peary, 1984). Indeed, major, minor and background characters are prominently disabled throughout the series, seemingly for a variety of narrative and atmospheric purposes.

However, it could also be argued that the *Mad Max* series offers an additional, broader social critique on disability. Significant social and cultural changes over the three and a half decades of the franchise have had great influence in this field, and many of the images of disability and trauma central to Max's post-apocalyptic desert wasteland could also be seen to represent these societal shifts in both social decline *and* rejuvenation. For example, the character Max Rockatansky transitioned from able-bodied masculinity in the first film to a limping, maddened road warrior in *The Road Warrior* and, by *Fury Road*, to a man haunted by guilt and hallucinations, often presenting as post-traumatic stress disorder (PTSD) but rediscovering himself and his humanity. By interrogating the role of these metaphors and representations of disability and trauma, this book offers an in-depth cultural analysis of the social critiques within *Mad Max*, drawing on production processes, textual analysis and reception studies (Fig. 1.1).

Fig. 1.1 Miller uses low-angle framing to emphasise impairment, especially lameness, afflicting Max and other characters in the series, often shown wearing braces or calipers to compensate for and minimise the disability

In this introductory chapter, we outline the origins and intentions of both critical trauma and critical disability studies, examining the sites of divergence and intersection. Disability studies, which arose from a civil rights platform, aims to position disability at the heart of discussions rather than at the margins. As an interdisciplinary field of scholarship, it seeks to explore models and theories that examine the social, political, cultural and economic factors that define disability and interrogate the way in which these are represented across time and place. Importantly, it challenges the view of disability as an individual deficit or defect that can be remedied solely through medical intervention, the so-called medical model of disability, and rather sets out to explore the social construction of disability in which disability is viewed as arising not from the body but rather from social and cultural barriers to society. This social model redefines disability as a problem with society, imposed on top of bodies, not as a problem existing within a damaged body and, as such, sometimes under-theorises the effects of impairment and trauma.

James Berger describes trauma studies and disability studies as "two of the most important new fields in the humanities" (Berger, 2004, p. 563). They have much in common, including a shared interest in representations of the body, in devastating injury and its lasting effects, and in the broad social and historical contexts of trauma and disability, respectively. Significantly for the humanities, both "focus intensively on problematics of representation" (Berger, 2004, p. 563). However, despite these commonalities, critical trauma and critical disability studies do not often collaborate in the production of new scholarship. Indeed, whilst trauma studies rarely considers disability, disability studies seems to avoid even mentioning trauma (Berger, 2004). Within a disability studies framework, trauma is often considered as falling within the domain of the medical model and, as mentioned above, critical disability studies challenges the assumption that disability is an individual deficit or defect that can be remedied solely through medical intervention and rather sets out to explore the social construction of disability. In pursuit of this aim, disability studies has therefore worked hard to "recast disability as something more than inherently traumatic or traumatizing" (Casper & Morrison, 2012).

Like disability studies, trauma studies—as an interdisciplinary field of enquiry seeking to explore social, historical and cultural influences—has undergone several stages. Just as disability studies recognises disability is culturally constructed, a humanities approach to trauma recognises and names trauma:

> not only as a condition of broken bodies and shattered minds, but also and primarily as a cultural object. In these framings, "trauma" is a product of history and politics, subject to reinterpretation, contestation and intervention. (Casper & Wertheimer, 2016)

With regard to the aforementioned medical versus social model argument, trauma studies emerged from the clinical study and treatment of traumatic injuries and is therefore more closely tied to the medical model than critical disability studies which was established through political activism. Further, although trauma studies has moved beyond purely clinical approaches to trauma (Ball, 2000), humanities approaches continue to think about trauma using a psychoanalytical approach to interpret the traumatic symptoms of the event experienced (Berger, 2004, p. 567). As a result, trauma studies focuses on the interpretation of language and the linguistic tropes used to describe these symptoms. The interpretation of metaphor is therefore, according to Berger, an important part of trauma studies as language is used to give meaning to "radically non-linguistic events" (p. 570).

By comparison, disability studies has tended to take a different approach to metaphor. Whereas trauma studies actively engages in making meaning from metaphor, disability scholars tend to be critical of this approach, alert to the pervasive use of negative disability metaphors that are socially damaging to disabled people (Berger, 2004, p. 570). Indeed, the tendency to use disability as background or for atmospheric purposes in cinema is well documented in disability studies (Norden, 1994). Analysis tends to suggest these characters draw on negative assumptions about disability in culture as a form of lazy storytelling (Longmore, 1987). Trauma studies recognises it is important to deal with historical traumas and investigates the use of cinematic metaphor in this process; however, disability studies is only recently coming to acknowledge the ways disability representation can, and does, open areas of cultural criticism, foregrounding potential for inclusion (Dolmage, 2014; Ellis, 2015).

However, disability theorists have recently begun to make calls for a return to the body, to a re-examination of the traditionally divisive medical versus social model standpoints. For example, Tobin Siebers makes an explicit link between disability and trauma via an investigation of disability aesthetics and the "corporeal substrata on which aesthetic effects are based" (Siebers, 2010, p. 1). Siebers follows the eighteenth-century German philosopher Alexander Baumgarten's notion that "[a]esthetics tracks the sensations that some bodies feel in the presence of other bodies" (Siebers, 2010, p. 1). Returning to the *Mad Max* series, just as Siebers suggests disability and trauma extend the possibilities of great art, Miller also invokes disability and trauma throughout the quartet to elicit an emotional response in the hopes of a social conversation about the limits of the human body. As such, these films are recognised in this vein as "finely calibrated to make their audience feel something, and to elicit an almost pre-conscious, primitive response" (Douglas, 2017). Indeed, with the release of the first film, Miller reflected on his approach to cinematic style as located in the embodied response of his audience in a 1979 interview with *Cinema Papers*:

> what we are doing in *Mad Max* is putting something on the screen for people to see and experience, which has the impact of being in a car accident. There is a commentary in *Mad Max*, and it would be nice to establish some sort of dialogue on the subject, but I don't think any film can do so. Films operate on emotions, not on rational thought. We don't understand anything that's very primitive and atavistic in our society; we don't understand sex and violence, because they are not functions of our intellect—they are functions of our biology. But we do know that the level of socially acceptable violent death in our society seems to be constant. (Miller, as cited in Beilby & Murray, 1979, p. 369)

Disability is invoked in these films as a central aesthetic concept, not only because it symbolises human variation but also because it represents the fragility of human beings and their susceptibility to dramatic physical and mental change. We echo Siebers' calls for a mutual recognition between both disability and trauma because "the capacity to be wounded, injured, or traumatized is not always considered a feature of disability, but it should be" (Siebers, 2010, p. 102). Similarly, theorists such as Casper and Morrison have also called disability studies to refocus attention on the body and the effects of impairment to both expand discussions of disability and productively connect disability and trauma studies (Casper & Morrison, 2012). In particular, the aforementioned under-theorisation of trauma is of concern to a key group of critical disability theorists (Kafer, 2016).

The medical model has therefore begun to emerge as a key source of tension within recent articulations of critical disability studies and the social model of disability. Alison Kafer (2013) admits to being both "critical of the medical model of disability" and "equally wary of a complete rejection of medical intervention" (Kafer, 2013, p. 4). Given that many disabled people engage with the medical model by actively seeking treatment or a cure for their disabling illness or chronic condition, Allegra Stout and Ariel Schwartz (2014) also question the ongoing separation of these two models (Stout & Schwartz, 2014). It is therefore increasingly being recognised that disability is not solely located in social practices. As Davidson explains:

> [t]he argument that disability is not lodged in the individual but in social barriers to full inclusion now seems a rather blunt instrument for describing the wide spectrum of disability experiences. (Davidson, 2016, p. 434)

Indeed, in 2008 Tobin Siebers recommended more in-depth consideration of the medical model as the next step in disability studies, calling for increased attention to the notion of complex embodiment:

> [t]he next step for disability studies is to develop a theory of complex embodiment that values disability as a form of human variation. The theory of complex embodiment raises awareness of the effects of disabling environments on people's lived experience of the body, but it emphasizes as well that some factors affecting disability, such as chronic pain, secondary health effects, and aging, derive from the body. (Siebers, 2008, p. 25)

A link between disability and trauma studies is therefore offered as one potential way forward for the social model of disability to rethink the impacts of impairment (Casper & Morrison, 2012). As Margaret Rose Torrell suggests:

> the denial of pain and loss in much work of disability studies is a main reason why theorists such as Siebers, Morrison and Casper, and Berger argue for a merger with trauma studies. The belief is that trauma studies' focus on pain and loss will provide disability studies an entrée into discussing such topics. (Torrell, 2016, p. 91)

Indeed, these calls for a more embodied understanding of disability are reinforced by Elizabeth J. Donaldson and Catherine Prendergast who draw disability scholars' attention to the necessity of refocusing on emotions (Donaldson & Prendergast, 2011). They argue that physical impairment has dominated disability studies to the extent that the field has "inherited damaging ableist assumptions of 'mind' that discourage a more robust consideration of emotion" (p. 130). Is this "return to the body" and the emotional turn in cultural theory, which a number of disability scholars appear to be calling for, an opportunity for disability and trauma studies to be drawn closer together? How can this be applied to film analysis? Certainly Miller's *Mad Max* series appears to be embracing a conversation between disability and trauma studies.

Outline

Following this introductory chapter, our book begins with Chap. 2, Trauma. This chapter details the previously unrecognised traumatic hauntings of Max, exemplified by his audio-verbal and visual hallucinations which manifest throughout *Fury Road* (2015) and other expressions in the preceding trilogy and align this representation with new cognitive psychiatric research challenging existing paradigms of PTSD (McCarthy-Jones & Longden, 2015; Steel, 2015; Waters & Fernyhough, 2017). Miller's cinematic expression of such traumatic symptomology will be shown to be uncannily prescient of these new research discoveries, writ large on the screen for global audiences.

Chapter 3, Disability, reviews the narrative function of the disabled characters which populate the world of *Mad Max*. The chapter applies Tobin Siebers' ideology of ability to these characters, emphasising the ways they imagine new worlds in which disability is valued as a form of diversity. While an elderly woman (Aunt May) with calipers on her legs caring for an intellectually disabled man in regional Australia in *Mad Max* adds to the isolation often invoked during this period of Australian filmmaking and reflects social concerns with deinstitutionalisation, the maimed and helpless masses congregating outside the citadel waiting for the similarly maimed but still powerful Immortan Joe to give them water, as well as the sickly War Boys inside, all make a broader social critique about the effects of war, political instability and resource shortage in *Fury Road*.

Gender is the focus of Chap. 4. *Mad Max: Fury Road* is often celebrated for embracing a strong feminist political agenda. From the original *Mad Max* to *Fury Road*, the series consciously plays with notions and representations of gendered sexuality and problematises conventions of masculinity and femininity, patriarchy and feminism, including the Warrior Woman of *Mad Max 2*, the matriarch Aunty Entity in *Beyond Thunderdome* and the hero Furiosa in *Fury Road*. We examine the franchise's evolution over decades as part of a long-standing tradition of female action heroes whose physical and emotional arcs prompt a questioning of traditional notions of both masculinity and femininity. For example, what has gone significantly unremarked in both the popular reviews and academic explorations of this franchise is Furiosa's disability. Furiosa *is* the Interceptor as her amputated arm merges with machines to render her the superior road warrior—she drives and shoots with the most accuracy. As such, this chapter considers the way disability intersects with gender throughout *Mad Max*, but especially within the characters of *Fury Road*, to offer a critique of both late capitalism and patriarchal society.

The structural and thematic resonance of mythology informs Chap. 5. When Tina Turner sang *We Don't Need Another Hero* over the end credits of *Mad Max: Beyond Thunderdome* (1985), it seemed that the trilogy had exhausted its heroic narrative trajectory. However, an application of Joseph Campbell's myth scholarship suggests George Miller understood that Max's journey remained incomplete and lacking resolution. As such, this chapter considers the cultural and cinematic myths of heroism, trauma and disability in *Fury Road* (2015) alongside Max's character transformation and questions of predeterminism and fate. It examines the influence of Campbell's "monomyth" across the three decades of the four films in order to reflect shifting international geopolitics—including petrochemical dependence and globalisation—sociocultural contexts and, significantly, the spectres of indigenous genocide, all resonating within our emergent epoch now widely understood as the Anthropocene.

Mad Max is an open-ended character upon which audiences have placed their own meanings. In Chap. 6, we conclude the book by considering the role of fandom in the longevity of the series, from queer readings and critiques, to *Mad Max* museums and fan gatherings in Australia, the USA and Japan, to several tumblr pages dedicated to the representation of disability and trauma within *Fury Road*. It is through these sites that the intersections between disability and trauma in *Fury Road*, and by extension the preceding films, are most clearly articulated.

This book is written as a brief provocation to encourage further work in the area. Our frames are necessarily tight and provide an entrée to each topic. Through this book, we suggest ways in which this study of the *Mad Max* franchise offers historical insights into both the mass-mediated representation of trauma and disability and how the series reflects and advances cultural understanding of these themes across its longitudinal production and reception. It is our hope this critical conversation will continue as *Mad Max* characters and mythology continue to evolve internationally across entertainment platforms, including in comics and games.

References

Ball, K. (2000). Introduction: Trauma and its institutional destinies. *Cultural Critique, 46*(46), 1–44. https://doi.org/10.2307/1354407

Beilby, P., & Murray, S. (1979). Production report: *Mad Max. Cinema Papers, 21*, 369.

Berger, J. (2004). Trauma without disability, disability without trauma: A disciplinary divide. *JAC, 24*(3), 563–582.

Casper, M. J., & Morrison, D. R. (2012). Intersections of disability studies and critical trauma studies: A provocation. *Disability Studies Quarterly, 32*(2). https://doi.org/10.18061/dsq.v32i2.3189

Casper, M. J., & Wertheimer, E. (Eds.). (2016). *Critical trauma studies: Understanding violence, conflict and memory in everyday life*. New York, NY: New York University Press.

Davidson, M. (2016). Cripping consensus: Disability studies at the intersection. *American Literary History, 28*(2), 433–453.

Dolmage, J. (2014). *Disability rhetoric* (1st ed.). Syracuse: Syracuse University Press.

Donaldson, E. J., & Prendergast, C. (2011). Introduction: Disability and emotion: "There's no crying in disability studies!". *Journal of Literary & Cultural Disability Studies, 5*(2), 129–135. https://doi.org/10.3828/jlcds.2011.11

Douglas, J. R. (2017). Great directors: George Miler. *Senses of Cinema, 83*. Retrieved from http://sensesofcinema.com/2017/great-directors/george-miller/#fn-30702-30702

Ellis, K. (2015). *Disability and popular culture: Focusing passion, creating community and expressing defiance*. Surrey, UK: Ashgate.

Kafer, A. (2013). *Feminist, queer, crip*. Bloomington, IN: Indiana University Press.

Kafer, A. (2016). Un/safe disclosures: Scenes of disability and trauma. *Journal of Literary & Cultural Disability Studies, 10*(1), 1–20. https://doi.org/10.3828/jlcds.2016.1

Longmore, P. (1987). Screening stereotypes: Images of disabled people in television and motion pictures. In A. Gartner & T. Joe (Eds.), *Images of the disabled, disabling images* (pp. 65–78). New York, NY: Praeger.

Mathews, S. (1984). *35mm dreams*. Ringwood, Vic: Penguin.

McCarthy-Jones, S., & Longden, E. (2015). Auditory verbal hallucinations in schizophrenia and post-traumatic stress disorder: Common phenomenology, common cause, common interventions? *Frontiers in Psychology, 6*, 1071. https://doi.org/10.3389/fpsyg.2015.01071

Norden, M. (1994). *The cinema of isolation: A history of physical disability in the movies*. New Brunswick: Rutgers University Press.

Peary, D. (1984). Directing Mad Max and the Road Warrior: An interview with George Miller. In D. Peary (Ed.), *OMNI's screen flights/screen fantasies* (pp. 279–286). New York, NY: Dolphin.

Siebers, T. (2008). *Disability theory*. Ann Arbor, MI: University of Michigan Press.
Siebers, T. (2010). *Disability aesthetics*. Ann Arbor, MI: University of Michigan Press.
Steel, C. (2015). Hallucinations as a trauma-based memory: Implications for psychological interventions. *Frontiers in Psychology, 6*, 1262. https://doi.org/10.3389/fpsyg.2015.01262
Stout, A., & Schwartz, A. (2014). It'll grow organically and naturally: The reciprocal relationship between student groups and disability studies on college campuses. *Disability Studies Quarterly, 34*(2). https://doi.org/10.18061/dsq.v34i2
Torrell, M. R. (2016). Interactions: Disability, trauma, and the autobiography. *Life Writing, 13*(1), 87–103. https://doi.org/10.1080/14484528.2016.1129572
Waters, F., & Fernyhough, C. (2017). Hallucinations: A systematic review of points of similarity and difference across diagnostic classes. *Schizophrenia Bulletin, 43*(1), 32–43. https://doi.org/10.1093/schbul/sbw132

CHAPTER 2

Trauma

Abstract Conventional film scholarship has largely eschewed the analysis of screen texts from psychiatric and cognitivist approaches to traumatic representation. This chapter considers the convergence of emerging research into post-traumatic stress disorder (PTSD) that challenges notions of psychotic behaviour (auditory, verbal and/or visual hallucinations—AVH) as aberrant amongst general PTSD sufferers. It aligns these findings with the recent global release of George Miller's rebooted *Mad Max: Fury Road* (2015). By undertaking a close textual reading of key film sequences, with reference to the broader narrative, film trauma scholarship and *Fury Road's* antecedents, this chapter suggests that this latest version of the *Mad Max* series strongly conforms to the new paradigms of PTSD symptomology.

Keywords Fury Road • Trauma • PTSD • Hallucination • Psychosis • Madness • Flashbacks

After a gestation of 30 years the latest *Mad Max* film (the fourth in the series) was met with unprecedented media anticipation (Watercutter, 2015) and, for fans worldwide, great expectations (see Chap. 5). *Mad Max: Fury Road* (2015) directed by George Miller lends itself to multiple readings—from the post-apocalyptic (see Chap. 4), to representations of disability (see Chap. 2), to its interpretation as a (post)feminist film (see Chap. 3), the latter garnering

M. Broderick, K. Ellis, *Trauma and Disability in Mad Max*,
https://doi.org/10.1007/978-3-030-19439-0_2

significant reactionary responses from some male bloggers and in social media memes (Clarey, 2015; Shaw-Williams, 2015). This chapter explores the quartet of the *Mad Max* movies as cinematic trauma texts, concentrating on the last instalment, *Fury Road*, as an exemplar of the symptomology of post-traumatic stress disorder (PTSD) and the emergence of new psychological research into the correlation and comorbidities of psychotic phenomena such as auditory, visual and/or verbal hallucinations (AVH). After a close textual reading of the opening sequence, *Fury Road* and its predecessors will be considered in terms of their proximity to and veracity in reflecting this emerging PTSD-AVH psychological paradigm.

Perhaps the most succinct definition of PTSD is that of a "pathological anxiety disorder resulting after exposure to a traumatic event" (Centre for the Treatment and Study of Anxiety, 2017). According to the fifth edition of the *Diagnostic and Statistical Manual of Mental Disorders* (DSM-5), PTSD is characterised by the following primary symptoms:

1. Direct or indirect exposure to a traumatic event, such as actual or threatened death, serious injury or sexual violence.
2. Recurrent recollections of the event as an intrusion or re-experiencing, including dreams, memories and prolonged distress or physical reactions to cues that resemble the traumatic event.
3. Fear and avoidance behaviour of people, places, thoughts, feelings or activities closely associated with the traumatic event.
4. Changes in mood and cognition including negative emotions or thoughts with exaggerated negative beliefs and self-blame for the traumatic event, detachment, disinterest and a reduced capacity for positive emotions.
5. Arousal and hyper-reactivity with an agitated state of constant wakefulness or alertness; being easily startled, irritable or aggressive; recklessness, sleep disturbances and difficulty concentrating.

Across *Mad Max*, *The Road Warrior* and *Beyond Thunderdome* numerous representations of trauma, both physical and mental, as well as its intersection with grief and anger responses are evident (Olatunji, Ciesirlski, & Tolin, 2010; McHugh, Forbes, Bates, Hopwood, & Creamer, 2012). In particular, many of the above symptoms of PTSD and AVH manifestly impact upon characters throughout the series, most notably the eponymous anti-hero (played by Mel Gibson in the first three films and by Tom

Hardy in the latest). Although there are hints of Max's mental and emotional instability before his family is slain—he fears becoming a "terminal crazy" and is described by others as "in a coma" and "like a zombie"—the highway patrolman channels his traumatic response towards vengeance and violence, with Johnny the Boy calling him "mad" at the finale of *Mad Max*. George Miller has affirmed:

> Mad, angry, crazy Max has become a full monster, the avenging demon (Miller, as cited in Peary, 1984, p. 284.)

Judith Herman (1992, p. 121) has proposed a schema for recognising "complex" PTSD symptoms where some trauma victims may alternate between "explosive anger" and the opposite, namely suppression and inhibition. Such oscillating responses are manifest in Max and others throughout the series. For example, in *The Road Warrior*, both leaders of opposing factions, Pappagallo and the Humungus, articulate empathy and understanding of traumatic legacies. Pappagallo, limping from a leg wound received during the battle at his refinery/compound, chides Max for not being the only survivor in the post-apocalyptic world who has "suffered". He berates Max, telling him the loss of his family doesn't "make him special" (see Chap. 3). Max responds to Pappagallo's taunting over his unreconciled trauma and grief in a violent outburst, striking the injured Pappagallo to the ground. Earlier, the mohawk biker Wez is shown distraught and vengeful (echoing Max's anger in *Mad Max*) after his male partner is killed by the Feral Kid's boomerang, yelling in rage to his fellow Dogs of War "We kill! We kill them!" The masked Humungus (a close-up revealing his hairless, disfigured and scarred skull) promptly restrains Wez in a headlock, consoling him with "I understand your pain. We've all lost someone we love". The exchange not only provides a narrative parallelism between opposing survivor camps, but typologically mirrors traumatic histories, both depicted and implied, from the original film to the sequel. In a 1984 interview with Danny Peary, director George Miller observed (Fig. 2.1):

> We invented a back story for every character. We imagined that the Humungus had been some kind of military man who'd been in a severe accident or explosion and suffered facial or head burns. He wore that mystifying mask as a form of intimidation and a sign of authority (Miller, as cited in Peary, 1984, p. 282–3.)

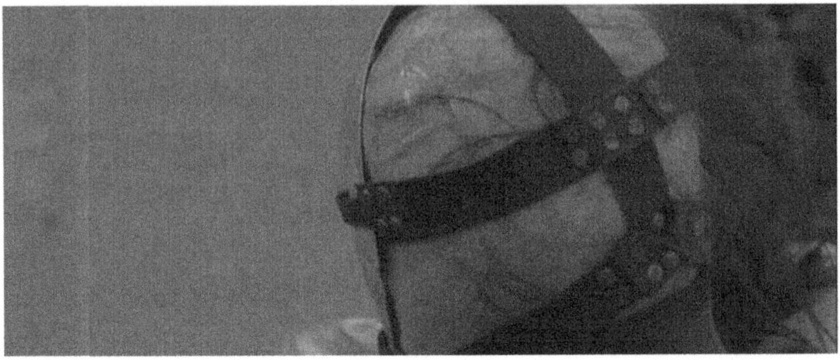

Fig. 2.1 A close-up of The Humungus (Kjell Nilsson) revealing scars across his (masked) skull, as he forcibly restrains and consoles mohawk Wez while acknowledging their shared grief and pain

Another key symptom of PTSD not specifically identified in the DSM-5, but noted by Herman (1992) as chronic and complex trauma, is alexithymia in the form of "psychogenic" or "selective" mutism, where the inability to express one's emotions is extended to inhibited speech (Dayer, Roulet, Maeder, & Deonna, 1998). This phenomenon usually occurs in children who stop speaking for some time as a result of traumatic experience or witnessing. Certainly, *The Road Warrior*'s Feral Kid exhibits this symptomology, although no physical or psychological impairment is explicitly presented. However, the closing narration of the film by an (unseen) elderly man is revealed to be that of the Feral Kid, related retrospectively from some future vantage point, suggesting that the child recovers his vocal capacity at a later time. Similarly, in *Beyond Thunderdome,* the so-called Lost Tribe of children (also referred to as the "waiting ones") who find refuge in Planet Earth, a deep ravine and verdant waterhole in the desert, includes a shamanistic character named Scroolose who is speechless and remains distant from the others, living in a cave above the gorge. His physical look is different; a shaved head crowned with dark pate of hair and white paint at the sides, and dark, hollowing eye make-up, appearing skull-like with a white talc covering his skin, anticipating the terminally-ill War Boys in *Fury Road.*

Until quite recently in the psychiatric/psychological literature concerning PTSD, there had been little research conducted to investigate the association between "hallucinations and the re-experiencing of a traumatic event" (Steel, 2015). However, clinical interventions for PTSD are now aimed at treating patients presenting with symptoms of *psychotic* disorders such as those experiencing hallucinations. Steel traces the aetiology of such manifestations back to Freud's 1936 analysis of the phenomenon, where hallucinations are pathologised as a "product of forgotten or repressed traumatic memories entering the conscious mind" (Freud, 1936; Freud, as cited in Steel, 2015).

As a result, fundamental to *Fury Road,* and much cultural representation, a "hallmark symptom" of PTSD is considered to be an "intrusive memory of a traumatic event, most likely in the form of a *visual image*" [our emphasis] (Steel, 2015). However, in reality, the most commonly considered intrusive sensory aberrations are via "auditory modality", namely hearing voices, something long associated with schizophrenia. Hence, research aimed at comprehending psychotic symptoms with respect to traumatic events has concentrated on aural phenomenon while psychological models of PTSD have primarily addressed "intrusive images" (Steel, 2015). The veracity of this distinction as a binary paradigm is now under active research and review (McCarthy-Jones & Longden, 2015).

Still, there have been noted exceptions. According to Hamner et al. (2000), such psychotic features are not uncommon in "combat veterans with chronic posttraumatic stress disorder" and may "reflect a distinct subtype". Amongst this cohort, the symptoms include "auditory and visual hallucinations and delusional thinking that is usually paranoid in nature". The authors suggest that these psychotic traits "may be underrecognized in chronic PTSD" due to under-reportage, or the misdiagnosis of "bizarre delusions characteristic of other psychoses" such as schizophrenia (Hamner et al., 2000).

For McCarthy-Jones and Longden, the phenomenology of AVH, or "hearing voices", is evident in both schizophrenics *and* sufferers of PTSD. Their research concludes that "the presence of AVH in schizophrenia is often associated with earlier exposure to traumatic/emotionally overwhelming events, as it is by definition in PTSD" rather than necessarily being a "direct re-experiencing" of the initiating trauma (McCarthy-Jones & Longden, 2015). Based on cognitive models of PTSD, these researchers suggest that the "reconstructive nature of memory may be able to account for the nature of these associations" involving both trauma and AVH, symptoms also brought on by "threat-hypervigilance and the individual's personal goals".

Recent political and social focus has been placed on the disablement of those considered to be the most able-bodied and masculine in society—

professional sports players, firefighters and military veterans (Derby, 2016). Veterans in particular are receiving significant attention with "a third to more than 50% of people exposed to military combat and captivity" meeting the criteria for PTSD (Derby, 2016). PTSD has been reclassified from an anxiety disorder to a new category of trauma and stress-related disorders with four diagnostic clusters—re-experiencing, avoidance, negative cognitions and mood and arousal. Max exhibits all the symptoms of PTSD identified by Derby throughout the four films:

> horrific or missing memories of the event, vivid dreams, flashbacks, constant reminders, distressing feelings, exaggerated blame and self-blame, social disconnect, decreased interest in activities and social interaction, reckless and aggressive behaviour, hyper-vigilance, and sleep disturbances. (Derby, 2016)

These symptoms which, from a critical disability perspective are all located in the body, have a profoundly disabling effect on an individual suffering PTSD even before, as Derby (2016) notes, one takes into consideration the "disabling sociocultural and personal impacts of ableism".

This diagnostic framework has great relevance for the escapades of Max in *Fury Road*. As a sole, nomadic PTSD scavenger in a desolate and hostile terrain, Max is necessarily hypervigilant; his survival and longevity depends on guarded watchfulness. Indeed, Miller's mise-en-scène and camerawork accentuates close-ups of Max as his eyes flash and dart about his surrounds, promptly evaluating his environment for any contingency, especially violence and flight response. According to the American Psychiatric Association (2013), such "hypervigilance for threat" is a characteristic consequence of trauma and a symptom of PTSD which has been observed as a causal trigger for some hallucinations. Thus, within the narrative of *Fury Road*, Max's hyper-awareness of his environment is matched by a propensity for heightened instinctual reaction and action.

Indeed, this form of auditory flashback associated with PTSD typically manifests as the "re-experiencing of auditions surrounding the trauma", something uncommon in schizophrenia, yet they can remain continuously present. In this sense, the psychotic phenomenon may present like schizophrenia, with long periods of hallucination, both aural and visual (Waters & Fernyhough, 2017). For example, sufferers of PTSD-AVH often have thematic hallucinations that "indirectly reflect the nature of the trauma". These can be audible, derogatory slurs that reference perceived failures or inadequacies of the subject (McCarthy-Jones & Longden, 2015). In *Fury Road* these demeaning imputations confront Max throughout the opening chase scene, evinced by the ghostly apparitions who accuse him with phrases such as "You let us die!"

Other researchers, such as Ehlers and Clark (2000), argue that "re-experiencing" in PTSD stems from memory intrusions, where the subject's traumatic experiences have not been successfully incorporated or consolidated into autobiographical memory. During traumatic exposure, the cognitive processes become "data-driven" rather than concept-driven, or "dissociative" as the input stimulus is not fully integrated. Such stimuli may not be recalled voluntarily, but can be triggered suddenly when elements associated with the original trauma are encountered (McCarthy-Jones & Longden, 2015).

Beyond Fury

The stated origins of *Mad Max*, both as lead character (cop Max Rockatansky) and as an eponymous movie marquee title, stem from director George Miller's pre-film career experience as a medical practitioner. Miller was troubled by the appalling injuries he would encounter from road trauma and based a number of the injuries in the *Mad Max* series on his clinical treatment of car crash victims. The filmmaker has noted that he witnessed "a lot of trauma from cars, and that did affect me [...] I wondered what it would be like if you were a cop [...] seeing it all the time" (Bravin, 2015). For example, Miller recounted that, as a young resident at a Sydney hospital, he was on call when five victims of a horrendous car crash were rushed into the Emergency Room. A young girl was brought in under a rubber blanket but he "couldn't even make out what should have been her legs, she was so badly crushed" (Galloway, 2016). Miller attempted repeatedly to inject intravenous fluid but he couldn't access a vein in her arm that was capable of taking the needle, so instead he inserted the IV directly into her neck. The doctor-filmmaker remembered that the girl was conscious throughout her ordeal:

> She kept saying, "Die me" [...] She was wheeled into the operating room and died that night. Eight years later, she came back in a dream. Her head was severed except for a flap of skin [and] she was saying "Die me!" I couldn't understand how she could talk. (Miller, as cited in Galloway, 2016)

While not attempting to pathologise Miller, his reflection regarding this case nevertheless speaks to a transference of the physical trauma—pulverised bones, muscles and organs—afflicting this young girl to the latent, psychological trauma evident in the director's own nightmare and in his patient's death plea. As such, it was experiences such as this which eventually became "the trigger" for the *Mad Max* series as "a way for me to deal with all that" (Miller, as cited in Bravin, 2015). Indeed, Miller based a number of the injuries in the series on his clinical treatment of car crash victims—for example, the real-life triage scenario outlined above is repeated with some variation in *Fury Road* where Max removes an IV needle and tube from his neck (he functions as a captive, mobile "blood bag") and later reinserts it to save Furiosa. Additionally, the repeated visitation to Max by a girl phantom in *Fury Road* may well also be Miller's cinematic expression to help exorcise his harrowing real-life memory.

Other personal anecdotes by Miller that attest to his own childhood trauma have also informed his film work, and many of these are manifest in sequences across the *Mad Max* quartet. In one revealing personal instance, Miller nearly drowned in a rural Queensland river while attempting to save another, older boy who had accidentally dragged him under the water. Miller lost consciousness but was rescued by a nearby adult who came on horseback. This near-fatal immersion finds expression in *Fury Road* in one vivid and unsettling scene early in the film which features Max being held under water by several men. With his mouth gagged and his eyes wide open, he suffers an intense hallucination in a reverse-shot depicting the phantom girl underwater, questioning and challenging him.

The filmmaker has also recollected having "night terrors" from age 11 at boarding school, repeatedly experiencing "feelings of having done something so irrevocable [...] you can never recover from it":

> I had a deep sense of terror. And there were always these strange little dreams, recurring dreams of a man on a horse riding across a desert landscape, and the landscape started to move and he got swallowed up. (Miller, as cited in Galloway, 2016)

Variations on this traumatic scenario have become a trope throughout the series. In *Fury Road* Max and his War Boy tormentor Nux are engulfed inside a gigantic sandstorm. Both are shown consumed by the sand, yet they emerge to fight again. In *The Road Warrior* the Gyro Captain surfaces menacingly from his hiding place beneath sand to try and trap Max (Mel Gibson). In *Mad Max Beyond Thunderdome* (1985) one of the sur-

Fig. 2.2 One of the Lost Tribe that Max and the other children cannot save, who is consumed by a desert sink-hole

viving children from the feral tribe is swallowed up inside a dune and, despite Max's efforts, the boy slowly submerges into the void. Such inundation and submersion is also presented as a means of torture in *Beyond Thunderdome* when the Underworld's diminutive mastermind (the top "half" of Master Blaster) is nearly suffocated by being dipped head-first into pig shit in a crowded sty at a subterranean methane farm (Fig. 2.2).

The newly rebooted *Mad Max* film opens with the following didactic (yet poetic) first-person narration: "My name is Max. My world is fire and blood". These terse words are immediately followed by an overlaid medley of voices:

Man 1: Why are you hurting these people?
Man 2: It's the oil stupid.
Man 3: Oil wars.
Man 4: We are killing for guzzoline.
Woman 1: The world is running out of water.

At the end of this verbal mash-up, Max reflects: "Once, I was a cop. A road warrior searching for a righteous cause". Later we come to understand that Max, despite his previous "righteous" intentions, is on a journey, like Furiosa, towards "redemption". The aural collage continues with:

Man 5: … to the terminal freak out point.
Man 6: [sounding uncannily like US President Ronald Reagan]: Mankind has gone rogue, terrorising itself.

A close-up view of black and white Cold War nuclear test footage shows trees being violently swept away, bending to and fro in the nuclear blast wave and inverse suction, under which a different male voice proclaims:
Another man: Thermonuclear skirmish.

In the background, the radioactive cackle of a Geiger counter underscores a series of ominous female voices:

Woman 2:	The earth is sour.
Woman 3:	Our bones are poisoned.
Woman 4:	We have become half-life.

The discourse economically relays the idea that Max inhabits a post-catastrophe environment, one unnaturally contaminated by radiation and other toxins that have leached their way into the ecology and the very marrow of humanity, metastasising into diseases, mutation, scars, birth defects and tumours evident in the remnant population, and first typified by a small, two-headed lizard that scuttles towards Max, which he deftly dispatches and eats. The scene simultaneously points to the effects of a disabling environment and the lived experience of disability and trauma.

In the background, unseen crows caw and Max continues: "As the world fell, each of us, in our own way, was broken. It was hard to know who was more crazy". A rapid cut follows to the opening, establishing shot of Max next to his car overlooking a desert. He continues narrating, claiming "me, or everyone else". This commentary serves to foreground his self-doubt and possible mania—and potentially that of the entire world. At this early point an audience might ponder, is Max delusional or pathological or, in the context of the phantom voices and archival imagery, is he, comparatively, sane?

As the camera cranes down from a vista of the panoramic wilderness before Max, an apparently non-diegetic girl's voice is heard with a reverberant echo saying "Hello ... where are you?" Max continues his monologic narration with "Here they come again. Worming their way into the black matter of my brain". Instantly, the cumulative effect of this preceding aural and visual montage of archival sound bites and imagery conveys an association that Max's introspective narration—and the suggestive apparition/hallucination of ghosts from his past—registers residual guilt over his survival at the expense of others, possibly those near and dear to him. The short opening sequence connotes that Max may well be suffering from PTSD or some form of psychosis. He is, after all, as the film title announces, "mad" Max. Yet he overtly expresses some anxiety about being "crazy" and is capable of wresting cognitive control and asserting agency by not letting the disembodied voices affect him, presumably by his understanding that they are imaginary or ghosts.

An ensuing pursuit by desert marauders (the War Boys) results in Max overturning his vehicle during a high-speed chase. Crawling out of his upturned car, dazed and disorientated—the camera appears to shudder but it is actually a rapid series of lap-dissolves that evokes concussion via a parallax effect—Max continues his voiceover, lamenting:

> I am the one who is haunted by the living and the dead. Hunted by scavengers. Haunted by those that I could not protect.

The statement is promptly followed by a cut to a "flashback" of a young girl running in front of an assembly of large trucks which is later revealed to be Immortan Joe's entourage. A quick cut presents an extreme close-up of the girl's eyes as she is run down, just like Max's partner and child in the original film from 1979.[1] The girl is prepubescent, with dark hair, wearing a dirty brown singlet. The instantaneous cut-away to a close-up of her eyes lasts only two frames, during which she is bathed in blue light preceded by a flash of white, resembling a lightning strike. Within a heartbeat, she is seen falling under one of the larger rigs. Another edit instantly returns us to the plight of Max, desperately trying to escape, crawling across barren ground. Given the dense visual kinesis of the action and rapid editing, audiences are left to ponder if the brief appearance of this girl is a flashback, hallucination or a supernatural visitation.

The unexpected and transient nature of this spectral imagery as fast montage is accompanied by a literal, diegetic flashback using the post-production conceit of white washouts and exaggerated sound effects to (initially) register a cognitively disorienting and defamiliarising eruption of mise-en-scène. A secondary flashback bathes the screen in a burst of overexposure, depicting an overhead crane shot that zooms down on Max as he leans over the fallen girl, blood streaming from her nose, apparently dead. Rapid flashes—again using white washout—return us to Max in the desert, crawling away from his trashed car while his pursuers jeer and laugh at his plight. This fast, repetitive flash engenders a cinematic/alternative

[1] This is not the only act of cinematic self-cannibalisation by Miller within the series. The *Mad Max* quartet repeatedly represents characters and narrative actions intertextually.

state of consciousness that mirrors Max's interior monologue of hauntings as he is finally captured by the marauders.

Max is next seen bound and stretched prostrate while his hair is shorn. A man with a weeping, ulcerated lower lip (the Organic Mechanic) uses a metal implement to write on the road warrior's back. Within the cauterised flesh we briefly glimpse phrases and words such as "O-negative", "high octane" and "universal donor", with the terms "psychotic" and "muzzled" readily legible. Other tattooed text notes that Max has good eyes, multiple scars and "genitals intact", all of which is burned onto his back (Fig. 2.3).

These hot welts resemble both the keloids afflicting Japanese atom bomb victims and the scarifying ceremonial incisions common amongst many indigenous peoples. According to Enid Schildkrout, such scarification is traditionally used to help with patient wellbeing and healing, sometimes transcending them from victim to survivor, where participants ritualistically redefine themselves by passing through symbolic death to rebirth (Schildkrout, 2004). Hence, while this sequence clearly depicts Max's body as manifesting the physical signs of trauma, it may also visibly signify the emotional and psychological traumas—for example the hauntings—afflicting Max and other remnants of the unspecified global catastrophe.

Fig. 2.3 Max's traumatic history is literally inscribed and seared into his flesh

Still prostrate, a hot metal brand is removed from a fire and about to be plunged onto Max's body but he breaks free and fights back. There follows a sped-up chase scene—what myth scholar Joseph Campbell has described in generic hero tales as "a lively, often comical pursuit" (Campbell, 1973, p. 196–97) akin to silent era *Keystone Cops* and exaggerated cartoon violence. Attempting to evade his captors by hanging overhead from cage-like bars, a cleanly shaven Max again encounters a "vision" of the girl, this time peering down at him from above. She asks him quizzically:

> Max? Is that you?
> Where were you?

Nonplussed, Max plunges into the water below as the girl's distorted voice echoes:

> Help us.
> Where were you?
> Where were you, Max?

Face down in the water, bound and gagged, Max is repeatedly confronted by the girl, now submerged beneath him in vivid close-up and reverse-shot (Fig. 2.4).

Fig. 2.4 One of Max's repeated, haunting apparitions (Coco Jack Gillies), "Worming their way into the black matter of [his] brain"

Distraught and confused, Max fends off his pursuers once more and runs through a lengthy tunnel, again encountering the phantom child who reproaches him, demanding "Where were you, Max?" As she walks determinedly towards him, the girl's face quickly distorts and morphs into a skull with hollowed black eye sockets. "Stop running" she commands, her voice muffled and warped in multiple overlays. Racing further along the tunnel Max encounters another "ghost", this time (apparently) an elderly indigenous Australian man, bearded and with grey hair, who berates Max with "You let us die!" The refrain is repeated quickly in succession as Max runs into other spectres—including a facially disfigured character seen later in the film—all chanting:

> You let us die.
> You let us die. Why?
> You promised to help us!
> Why?

On approach the respective male and female heads and bodies are transformed into skulls and skeletons as a frantic Max runs "through" them only to once again confront the girl in extreme close-up.

Despite the elapsed time of this stunning pre-title sequence running for less than five minutes, the frenetic nature of the montage, rapid shot-ratio, furious musical score and jumbled verbal and aural soundscape all enable an overwhelming, vertiginous identification with Max, something further enhanced by the film's privileging of his phenomenological and narrative point of view.

The PTSD evident in Max is only one aspect of *Fury Road*'s character pathology. Throughout the series, Max is subject to multiple scenes of brutal violence, including a gunshot trauma to his leg and surviving a number of ferocious car crashes and near-death experiences. However, we are only permitted the privileged point of view in flashback sequences specifically from Max's personal orientation.[2] In *Fury Road*, no other character is afforded an internal monologue by which to assess their psychological motivations or introspective ruminations. We do not see nor hear Furiosa recount a traumatic history based on her disfigurement, nor

[2] It could be argued that the Feral Kid's narration as an old man in *The Road Warrior* can be interpreted as a retrospective trauma narrative, particularly since we see him being taken away as a child against his will (echoing Australia's Indigenous Stolen Generation) and looking back in anguish at Max, who fails to intervene.

is there any implied sympathy or sentimentalising over those with physical, let alone psychological, scarring. For example, Furiosa is introduced to audiences while viewed from behind, a steadicam following her in tight close-up, focused on the raised, branded scar on the back of her neck denoting her status as Imperator. Only as she advances and corporally occupies much of the screen frame does it become apparent that her left arm is missing and has been replaced by a crude metallic prosthesis.

Similarly, when Nux waxes lyrical about the glory of conflict and death in battle, awaiting an afterlife in Valhalla, the young women berate him. They refer to Nux as nothing but "battle fodder" and call Immortan Joe a "lying old man" who had "his logo seared on our backs" as "breeding stock". Despite the War Boy's dogmatic protests, the women retort by foregrounding pervasive, patriarchal violence:

Splendid:	"Battle fodder!"
Nux:	No, I am awaited!
Capable:	You're an old man's battle fodder! Killing everyone and everything!
Nux:	We're not to blame!
Splendid:	Then who killed the world?

This unanswered question from the visibly pregnant "breeder" Splendid reinforces the earlier image of graffiti scrawled within Immortan Joe's cavernous domestic vault-space where he keeps his "wives" captive as his sole "property".

Trauma Cinema(s)

Clinical definitions of trauma frequently separate the occurrence of an event or experience as opposed to its aftermath—that is, as a belated manifestation—thereby conceptualising trauma as a "kind of memory". Most clinicians also concur that this is an *exceptional* form of memory—not one created by symbols or narrative, but something closer to the scaring induced by an injury, consistent with the Greek etymology of "trauma" meaning "wound" (Traverso & Broderick, 2010, p. 6). In her 2005 monograph, Janet Walker has cogently defined "trauma cinema" as:

> a group of films that deal with a world-shattering event or events, whether public or personal [...] those that deal with traumatic events in a nonrealist

> mode characterized by disturbance and fragmentation of the film's narrative and stylistic regimes. (Walker, 2005, p. 19)

Hence, by this analysis, trauma films depart from the "narratological illusionist system" of classical Hollywood realism and deviate from traditions of mimetic audience identification enhancing verisimilitude. For Walker such films counter the classical paradigm by "disremembering". They create novel modes of presenting reality opaquely and obliquely "by looking to mental processes for inspiration, and by incorporating self-reflexive devices" that call attention to the history of audio-visual representation (Walker, 2005, p. 19). While *Fury Road* is mostly dependent upon classical Hollywood narrative, it nevertheless foregrounds its formal construction and production via hyper-realist interventions, for example, the kinetic momentum and trajectory of its chase sequences and the imaginative evocation of alternate states of consciousness.

Walker maintains that trauma films "are by definition a generation removed from the catastrophes they depict, and their audiences may be a generation removed from the original sufferers" (Walker, 2005, p. 193). In the case of the *Mad Max* films, given the series' reliance on an obvious temporal shift into the (near) future, this generation of viewers cannot help but be removed from the catastrophic scenarios on display as they have quite literally not yet transpired. However, the historical backdrop of geopolitics depicted in the archival auras that introduce *Fury Road* (and *The Road Warrior*) suggests either a consequence or the culmination of neo-liberal capitalism at the end of history. Apart from flashbacks, hauntings and sparse character recollections, the "original sufferers" of the undefined apocalypse are cinematic phantoms inhabiting a projected/anticipated future.

Coinciding with the global release of *Fury Road*, a number of works emerged linking ecology, trauma and movies. E. Ann Kaplan has continued her analysis of screen trauma in *Climate Trauma* (2015) where she suggests that dystopian cinema and fiction that foresees the future creates in audiences a *pre*-traumatic "anticipatory anxiety" (p. 217):

> cultures may now be entering a new era in which pretrauma is pervasive in the public sphere. In this new era, media of all kinds [...] offer catastrophic future scenarios. In these scenarios, audiences are invited to identify with future selves in uncertain, dangerous, and ultimately unsustainable worlds. Such identifications result in a pretraumatized population, living with a

sense of an uncertain future and an unreliable natural environment. My hope is that, instead of being passively terrified, audiences will begin to understand dystopian scenarios as warning humans of what they must, at all costs, avoid. (p. 225)

As curious as this globally pathologising speculation might be, it largely eschews substantial historical precedent (Kaplan, 2015, p. 837). It suffers too much from what Frank Kermode described as the perennial "sense of an ending", a common apocalyptic perspective from those "in the middest" (1967, 1995). For example, the long-studied cultural and psychosocial anxieties generated by nuclear fears (e.g. Lifton, 1967; Kovel, 1983; Boyer, 1985; Weart, 1998) and expressed in international film, media and other texts (see Nuttall, 1968; Broderick, 1991; Perine, 1998; Zeman & Amundson, 2004) have incessantly served as warnings of immediate and long-term ecological catastrophe on a planetary scale.[3] The *Mad Max* series and *Fury Road*, in particular, are but one such example of this subgenre of future dystopian cinema, dating back to *The Comet* (1910) and beyond (Fig. 2.5).

Fig. 2.5 Unknown characters in *Fury Road* on stilts traverse the toxic wasteland that was once the "Green Place" in a medievalesque composition evoking artists Bruegel and Bosch, while merging iconography of disability with eco-trauma

[3] Numerous works by psychologists as far back to Carl Jung in the 1950s have specifically addressed such traumas and anxieties. Other examples include works by Robert Lifton, John E. Mack and Sibylle Escalona.

Mark Steven's insightful 2015 essay on "eco-trauma cinema" from an Australian perspective finds the narratives of the *Mad Max* (up to then) trilogy require "external horror to resonate with internal trauma". This is particularly emblematic in the sequence where Max's family is run down by a biker gang and he then sets about wreaking merciless vengeance (Steven, 2015, p. 78). For Steven, Australian cinema in general—and the *Mad Max* films in particular—resonate with unresolved traumatic tensions, oscillating between (post-colonial) place and the individual, gendered character:

> By refracting distinctly Australian violence through psychological preconditions, forcing connections between the internal and the external real, the psyche is itself positioned as a product of the evolutionary habitation, conflating external shock with internal anxiety so as to make sense of the former, awaken the latter and to thereby deliver eco-trauma. One of the major outcomes of [*Mad Max*] is a specifically Australian idea of character, stretched between narrative and topography, crystallised through psychology, and [...] spilt along the lines of sexual difference. (Steven, 2015, p. 78)

Steven's eco-trauma perspective synthesises and advances the landmark work on "traumascapes" by Maria Tumarkin (2005) and the "shocking representation" of trauma in national cinemas outlined by Adam Lowenstien (2005) which, as a methodology, may provide a fruitful approach to the *Mad Max* series by addressing what have elsewhere been identified as "topographies of trauma" (Broderick, 2010).

Conclusion

This chapter has considered new developments in the understanding of PTSD and AVH, a theme and trope readily apparent in, and boldly imagined by, George Miller's reboot of the *Mad Max* franchise. Further research remains to be undertaken into other aspects of PTSD and related traumatic representation across the series, such as concepts of survivor guilt, envy, denial and avoidance. In the pages to follow we note, however, that many of these "symptoms" are evident in the narratives, characterisations and application of aesthetics to film style.

References

American Psychiatric Association. (2013). *Diagnostic and statistical manual of mental disorders* (5th ed.). Washington, DC: American Psychiatric Publishing. https://doi.org/10.1176/appi.books

Boyer, P. (1985). *By the bomb's early light: American thought and culture at the dawn of the atomic age*. New York, NY: Pantheon.

Bravin, J. (2015, May 14). George Miller returns to his personal wasteland in *Mad Max: Fury Road. Wall Street Journal.* Retrieved from https://blogs.wsj.com/speakeasy/2015/05/14/george-miller-returns-to-his-personal-wasteland-in-mad-max-fury-road/

Broderick, M. (1991). *Nuclear movies.* Jefferson, NC: McFarland & Co.

Broderick, M. (2010). Topographies of trauma, dark tourism and world heritage: Hiroshima's Genbaku Dome. *Intersections: Gender and Sexuality in Asia and the Pacific, 24.* http://intersections.anu.edu.au/issue24/broderick.htm

Campbell, J. (1973). *The hero with a thousand faces.* Princeton, NJ: Princeton University Press.

Centre for the Treatment and Study of Anxiety. (2017). *Post-traumatic stress disorder.* Department of Psychiatry, University of Melbourne. Retrieved from http://www.med.upenn.edu/ctsa/ptsd_symptoms.html

Clarey, A. (2015, May 11). Why you should not go see *Mad Max: Feminist Road. Return of the Kings.* Retrieved from http://www.returnofkings.com/63036/why-you-should-not-go-see-mad-max-feminist-road

Dayer, A., Roulet, E., Maeder, P., & Deonna, T. (1998). Post-traumatic mutism in children: Clinical characteristics, pattern of recovery and clinicopathological correlations. Retrieved from https://www.ncbi.nlm.nih.gov/pubmed/10726832

Derby, J. (2016). Virtual realities: The use of violent video games in U.S. military recruitment and treatment of mental disability caused by war. *Disability Studies Quarterly, 36*(1). Retrieved from http://dsq-sds.org/article/view/4704/4209

Ehlers, A., & Clark, D. M. (2000). A cognitive model of posttraumatic stress disorder. *Behaviour Research and Therapy, I*(4), 319–345.

Freud, S. (1936/1975). A disturbance of memory on the Acropolis. In S. Freud (Ed.), *The standard edition of the complete psychological works of Sigmund Freud* (Vol. 22, pp. 239–248). London, UK: Hogarth Press.

Galloway, S. (2016, May 10). *Mad Max* director George Miller is way too sane to be a mad genius. *The Hollywood Reporter.* Retrieved from http://www.hollywoodreporter.com/features/mad-max-director-george-miller-889872

Hamner, M. B., Frueh, B. C., Ulmer, H. G., Huber, M. G., Twomey, T. J., Tyson, C., et al. (2000). Psychotic features in chronic posttraumatic stress disorder and schizophrenia: Comparative severity. *Journal of Nervous & Mental Disease, 188*(4), 217–221.

Herman, J. (1992). *Trauma and recovery: The aftermath of violence – From domestic abuse to political terror.* New York, NY: Basic Books.

Kaplan, E. A. (2015). *Climate trauma: Foreseeing the future in dystopian film and fiction.* New Brunswick, NJ: Rutgers University Press.

Kermode, F. (1967). *The sense of an ending.* New York, NY: Oxford University Press.

Kermode, F. (1995). Waiting for the end. In M. Bull (Ed.), *Apocalypse theory and the ends of the world* (pp. 252–263). Oxford, UK: Blackwell.

Kovel, J. (1983). *Against the state of nuclear terror*. London, UK: Pan.

Lifton, R. J. (1967). *Death in life*. New York, NY: Penguin.

Lowenstein, A. (2005). *Shocking representation: Historical trauma, national cinema, and the modern horror film*. New York, NY: Columbia University Press.

McCarthy-Jones, S., & Longden, E. (2015). Auditory verbal hallucinations in schizophrenia and post-traumatic stress disorder: Common phenomenology, common cause, common interventions? *Frontiers in Psychology, 6*, 1071. https://doi.org/10.3389/fpsyg.2015.01071

McHugh, T., Forbes, D., Bates, G., Hopwood, M., & Creamer, M. (2012). Anger in PTSD: Is there a need for a concept of PTSD-related posttraumatic anger? *Clinical Psychology Review, 32*(2), 93–104.

Nuttall, J. (1968). *Bomb culture*. New York, NY: Delta.

Olatunji, B. O., Ciesirlski, B. G., & Tolin, D. F. (2010). Fear and loathing: A meta-analytic review of the specificity of anger in PTSD. *Behavior Therapy, 41*(1), 93–105.

Peary, D. (1984). Directing Mad Max and the Road Warrior: An interview with George Miller. In D. Peary (Ed.), *OMNI's screen flights/screen fantasies* (pp. 279–286). New York, NY: Dolphin.

Perine, T. A. (1998). *Film and the nuclear age: Representing cultural anxiety*. New York, NY: Garland Publishing.

Schildkrout, E. (2004). Inscribing the body. *Annual Review of Anthropology, 33*, 319–344.

Shaw-Williams, H. (2015, May 12). *Mad Max: Fury Road* consultant Eve Ensler calls it a 'Feminist Action Film'. *Screen Rant*. Retrieved from http://screenrant.com/mad-max-fury-road-eve-ensler-feminism/

Steel, C. (2015). Hallucinations as a trauma-based memory: Implications for psychological interventions. *Frontiers in Psychology, 6*, 1262. https://doi.org/10.3389/fpsyg.2015.01262

Steven, M. (2015). Great southern wounds: The trauma of Australian cinema. In A. Narine (Ed.), *Eco-trauma cinema* (pp. 72–87). London, UK: Routledge.

Traverso, A., & Broderick, M. (2010). Interrogating trauma: Towards a critical trauma studies. *Continuum: Journal of Media & Cultural Studies, 24*(1), 1–13.

Tumarkin, M. (2005). *Traumascapes: The power and fate of places transformed by tragedy*. Melbourne, VIC: Melbourne University Press.

Walker, J. (2005). *Trauma cinema: Documenting incest and the holocaust*. Berkeley, CA: University of California.

Watercutter, A. (2015, May 14). *Mad Max: Fury Road* was worth waiting 30 years for. *Wired*. Retrieved from https://www.wired.com/2015/05/mad-max-fury-road-review/

Waters, F., & Fernyhough, C. (2017). Hallucinations: A systematic review of points of similarity and difference across diagnostic classes. *Journal of Psychoses and Related Disorders: Schizophrenia Bulletin, 43*(1), 32–43. Retrieved from https://academic.oup.com/schizophreniabulletin/article/43/1/32/2549013/Hallucinations-A-Systematic-Review-of-Points-of

Weart, S. (1998). *Nuclear fear: A history of images.* Cambridge, MA: Harvard University Press.

Zeman, S. C., & Amundson, M. A. (2004). *Atomic culture: How we learned to stop worrying and love the bomb.* Boulder, CO: University of Colorado Press.

CHAPTER 3

Disability

Abstract Major, minor and background characters are prominently disabled throughout the *Mad Max* series seemingly for a variety of narrative and atmospheric purposes. However, importantly, these characters are never represented as DIS-abled—their visible, physical impairments do not prevent them from functioning productively in the futuristic world, nor are they ridiculed or otherwise marginalised by their community. In fact, many have highly specialised capacities that are crucial to a post-apocalyptic world. Further, perhaps due to the prevalence of disability throughout the *Mad Max* films, characters' impairments are rarely mentioned as part of the overall narrative. This is particularly noticeable as the world descends further into (post-)apocalypse and increasing numbers of impaired bodies populate and attempt to rebuild it.

Keywords Critical disability studies • Social critique • Impairment • Ideology of ability • Complex embodiment

Following on from the in-depth analysis of the clinical symptoms of Max's post-traumatic stress disorder (PTSD) as it relates to film language in the previous chapter, this chapter seeks to advance a critical conversation between the oftentimes conflicting roles of critical trauma and disability studies via the *Mad Max* series of films. Filmmakers have long been accused of drawing on metaphors of disability to visually communicate information

M. Broderick, K. Ellis, *Trauma and Disability in Mad Max*,
https://doi.org/10.1007/978-3-030-19439-0_3

about characters' internal, seemingly traumatic, worlds. For example, Max's leg brace in *The Road Warrior*, *Beyond Thunderdome* and briefly in *Fury Road* could be read as symbolic of his internal trauma. However, drawing on Siebers' (2010) ideology of ability and theory of complex embodiment, the chapter re-evaluates Miller's contribution to representations of disability and trauma throughout the series. Siebers offers the concept of the ideology of ability, firstly to understand the way society and culture exhibit a preference for able-bodiedness as a marker of what it means to be human and, secondly, to identify criticisms that arise in response to this essentialising agenda. Applying this approach to film analysis as a critical conversation between trauma and disability studies advances disability analysis of cinematic texts.

As the discussion of Max's symptomology in the previous chapter illustrates, social and biological factors work together to create the experience of disability. Approaching this construction from both a trauma studies and disability studies perspective, we recognise that the image of the disabled body and its impairments in cinema perform a double function:

> The disabled body is at once a symbol of the trauma of modern life and a call to discover a more inclusive and realistic conception of culture, one that recognizes the fragility as well as the violence of human existence. (Siebers, 2010, p. 103)

However, increasingly, the aforementioned strict separation of the medical and social models of disability has again been a source of tension. As such, several theorists recommend taking a trauma studies approach to disability, embodiment and human variation as a potential area of growth for disability studies. In this approach, the body itself, which disability studies has worked to shift focus away from, is recommended as the site at which this merger between disability and trauma studies could take place (Casper & Morrison, 2012). Margaret Rose Torrell observes that disability studies tends to disavow the experience of pain and loss and posits that trauma studies' focus on these embodiments will "provide disability studies an entrée into discussing such topics" (p. 91). This is particularly important given cinema's role in reimagining and re-enacting traumatic events and histories. As Traverso and Broderick explain, "questions about the impulse to behold and depict both the suffering of others and of the self, as well as more general questions about the ontological status of the representation of trauma, have increasingly been raised within intersecting, inter-disciplinary fields of study over the past two decades" (Traverso &

Broderick, 2010, p. 3). Therefore, while critical disability studies has tended to locate this cultural impulse in the domain of ableist reflex, a consideration of Siebers' complex embodiment offers the opportunity for new analytical insight.

Tobin Siebers begins *Disability and the Theory of Complex Embodiment: For Identity Politics in a New Register* by identifying two contradictory cultural approaches taken to the body. Firstly, the idea that bodies do not matter to who we are and, secondly, the notion that the human body must be perfected. The ready embrace of these contradictory approaches to the body, Siebers argues, "reveals that our thinking is steeped in ideology" (Siebers, 2013, p. 279). This "ideology of ability" exhibits a preference for able-bodiedness to define humanness:

> The ideology of ability is at its simplest the preference for ablebodiedness. At its most radical, it defines the baseline by which humanness is determined, setting the measure of body and mind that gives or denies human status to individual persons. (Siebers, 2013, p. 279)

This ideology is so deeply embedded in our social practices and institutions that it is difficult to identify or interrogate. It has become naturalised and normalised, yet ability is and has always been a myth (see Kumari Campbell, 2009)—humans are vulnerable as we are all at risk of disease, injury, natural disaster or man-made catastrophe. While the ideology of ability and the cultural capital ascribed to the normate constructs disability as abnormal, disability is a "natural form of human variation and diversity" to be accommodated, not eliminated (Garland-Thomson, 2015). As Jennifer Gagnon explains, "as long as being human means also to be embodied, it is obvious that disability will be central to the human experience" (Gagnon, 2016, p. 338).

However, disability is typically culturally invoked as a synonym for exclusion. Ability, by comparison, signifies value. The value of human life itself is called into question only when someone is disabled. Yet disability theorists are increasingly recognising that ability is just as socially constructed as disability (Kumari Campbell, 2009; McRuer, 2006; Siebers, 2013). In particular, an aesthetic of compulsory able-bodiedness (McRuer, 2006) dominates film and television. For Petra Kuppers, disability is a readable sign in cinema; it becomes the "symptom of trauma". While Max's leg brace in *The Road Warrior* is an example of this readable sign, its limited appearances in *Beyond Thunderdome* and *Fury Road* do not suggest that the disability or trauma has vanished, rather that Max's trauma has been internalised and now manifests as PTSD.

Socio-cultural conceptions of what it means to be human are at the centre of the ideology of ability. This ideology seeks a clear binary between disability and ability, human and not human, as well as extraordinary bodies and the notion of the normative (see Garland-Thomson, 1997). However, there is no normative body in *Mad Max*. In the first film, men are initially tenuously constructed as the normative, with women and children clearly constructed as exposed on the roads. However, even these men are vulnerable. The assault on Goose triggers Max to quit his job, and the death of his son and wife ultimately push him over the edge, towards becoming the "terminal crazy" he fears. However, as the series progresses, his increasing PTSD is his last connection to humanness—he is haunted by the people he's let down.

Further, while the ideology of ability continues to have negative consequences for people with disabilities, it can never be fully reconciled. The contradictions within and the workings of this ideology also facilitate the creation of critical social locations, with disability at the centre of the ideology of ability. For example, critical disability theorists often locate cinematic representations of disability within the domain of fear of disablement. Paul Longmore suggests that, in film, the possibility of disability is an unspoken anxiety which, to be neutralised, must be stigmatised, shunned and destroyed:

> Popular entertainment depicting disabled characters allude to these fears and prejudices or address them obliquely or fragmentarily, seeking to reassure us about ourselves. (Longmore, 1987, p. 66)

While such an approach has yielded important cultural insights and demonstrated the ways representations reference prior representations, it neglects to consider history and tends to essentialise the motivations of those producing the texts or reduce these to internalised ableism. The result is a partial analysis that does not go beyond the level of representation to consider "the historical and cultural circumstances of the people who created them" (Bogdan, 2012).

From *Mad Max* to *Fury Road*

For Miller, the fear of disablement represented in *Mad Max* is not unspoken or unconscious, nor is it stigmatised. While critical disability studies remains concerned over cinema perpetuating a fear of disability and for locating disability outside the bounds of normality, Miller admits in interviews about his motivations for creating *Mad Max* to a desire to interrogate the disabling impacts of trauma as a vehicle for social critique. As a former emergency doctor, Miller reflects on his use of road trauma as a metaphor for broader social decline: "it occurred to me that the kind of degeneracy on the roads was indicative of a kind of general social degeneracy" (Blowen, 1985). Miller's directorial influences are firmly located in his experiences as an emergency room doctor and within the Australian car culture of his youth where he witnessed significant road trauma:

> Working in the hospital I had developed a morbid fascination with the autocide we practise in our society: every weekend I'd see so many young people who'd been killed, or maimed for life, on the roads. You'd see the road toll in the paper on Monday morning and it was accepted with a shrug. It was almost like a weekly ritual, with people being randomly selected out as victims, as sacrifices to the car and the road. (Miller, as cited in Mathews, 1984, p. 236)

This comment from Miller draws on a key issue within critical disability studies—personal tragedy. As Petra Kuppers explains, "the experience of disability is often figured as a traumatic personal history, culturally marked as 'private' tragedy" (Kuppers, 2008). Yet, as Miller explains, while socially accepted as random personal tragedy, the road trauma he witnessed as both a doctor and living in car obsessed regional areas in Australia is a culturally created phenomenon for which we must take collective responsibility. *Mad Max* could therefore be read as making a critique of this culture. Disability features heavily, both prior to and following the onset of Max's traumatic loss of his family in *Mad Max*. These disabled bodies are a readable sign throughout the films that incite discomfort, a sense of impending doom and, paradoxically, occasional humour. This is not unique to the disabled body, however; each character encountered in the wasteland of the *Mad Max* franchise creates a kind of aesthetic nervousness (cf Quayson, 2007) for Max and the audience.

Indeed, the series offers no reassurance about its fear of disablement and the four films critique the ideology of ability by interrogating the preference for able-bodiedness evident in cinematic representation. This seems to follow Siebers' argument that disability and trauma is at the centre of what it means to be human:

> Human life confronts the overwhelming reality of sickness, injury, disfigurement, enfeeblement, old age, and death. Natural disasters, accidents, warfare and violence, starvation, disease and pollution of the natural environment attack human life on all fronts, and there are no survivors. (Siebers, 2013, p. 278)

Indeed, a cursory analysis of *Mad Max* reveals that bodies are fragile, even those that typically signify able-bodied masculinity. For Tom O'Regan, the first three films display an almost "hysterical anxiety" about the vulnerability of the male body:

> If *Mad Max* conjured up an everyday murderousness this was probably due to its carnival of flesh and body. At its heart, *Mad Max* was a story of mutilation, disempowerment and re-empowerment. Its maiming was carefully choreographed: a hand missing here, a limb there, a leg in a plaster, a body beneath a tent in too appalling a shape to be seen. Thus the film inscribed upon the male bodies on screen an almost hysterical anxiety—a fear of literal and symbolic castration. Max's body bears the marks of his journey. (O'Regan, 2005, p. 96)

Max's masculinity is therefore at stake (see Chap. 4). While each film could be read as a stand-alone cultural commentary of their respective social periods, when taken together they reveal definite thematic and narrative choices that are repeated across all four films. As Ato Quayson explains, a consideration of disability across an author's body of work provides the opportunity for a deeper investigation of disability:

> When the various references to disability and to disability representation are seen within the broad range of an individual writer's work, it helps to foreground hitherto unacknowledged dimensions of their writing and, in certain cases, this can even lead to a complete re-evaluation of critical emphasis. (Quayson, 2007)

As discussed, George Miller explicitly notes the fragility of human embodiment as motivation for *Mad Max*. He places disability at the centre of his critique. Siebers also recommends foregrounding disability as a way to end the dominance of the ideology of ability:

> Disability creates theories of embodiment more complex than the ideology of ability allows, and these many embodiments are each crucial to the under-

> standing of humanity and its variations, whether physical, mental, social or historical. (Siebers, 2013, p. 279)

Disability is used throughout *Mad Max* to interrogate what it means to be human and to foreground diversity as integral to hope for the future. Disabled characters throughout the four films contribute to their communities and adapt their own specialised technologies to compensate for the effects of their impairments. Their impairments are implied to be the direct result of the warfare and violence that caused the apocalypse. As the world declines and rebuilds throughout these films, the social construction of disability in the first two films has reverted to Vic Finkelstein's first stage of disability where disabled people existed on the margins and contributed to society through their own individualised technologies adapted to suit their specific bodily requirements (see Finkelstein, 1980; see also Chap. 5 for a discussion of disability, impairment and prosthesis in antiquity). However, rather than move through stage 2, the establishment of able-bodied normality, *Beyond Thunderdome* and *Fury Road* move straight to Finkelstein's third stage where mastery over individualised technology facilitates the re-inclusion of people with disability. As Fletcher and Primack observe, *Fury Road* in particular foregrounds a "turning away from a disabling understanding of present conditions through new practices that do not impede survival" (Fletcher & Primack, 2017, p. 351). Indeed while disability symbolism is integral to Miller's dramatisation of fear and optimism, and several visibly disabled characters populate the *Mad Max* quartet, they are never represented as DIS-abled. Their visible, physical impairments do not prevent them from functioning productively in the futuristic world, nor are they ridiculed or otherwise marginalised by their community. In fact, many have highly specialised capacities that are crucial to a post-apocalyptic world. While disability is common throughout *Mad Max*, characters' impairments are rarely mentioned as part of the overall narrative. This is particularly noticeable as the world descends further into (post-)apocalypse and increasing numbers of impaired bodies populate and attempt to rebuild it.

The notion of metaphor is important to both disability and trauma studies yet is approached in opposing ways. For trauma studies, the interpretation of metaphor is significant because language is used to give meaning to "radically non-linguistic events" (Berger, 2004, p. 570). Cinema, likewise, while not classically linguistic as such does have a visual language. For example, Miller describes his approach to filmmaking as visual and observes that audiences have become very adept at decoding cinematic language (Rodriguez, 2015). Throughout the four *Mad Max* films he draws on existing mythological and cinematic symbolism and metaphor (see Chap. 5) to offer "a vivid dramatisation of our worst fears [and] an expression of our most fearfully optimistic dreams" (Hassler-Forest, 2017, p. 306).

The *Mad Max* films connect trauma, the apocalypse and a critical understanding of disability. Each begins by locating the world in a post-apocalyptic future where bodies and minds are irrevocably damaged. The original *Mad Max* begins with the caption "a few years from now" dissolving into a desolate scene of highway patrol surveying a "high fatality" area, Anarchy Road. The subsequent films in the series also attempt to fill in some of the exposition and origins of the apocalypse that were omitted from the first film, with stock footage and voiceovers of children Max has met in his wanderings. For example, *Fury Road* begins with Max's voiceover: "As the world fell … each of us, in our own way, was broken. It was hard to know who was more crazy: Me … or everyone else".

The *Mad Max* films are a work of cultural criticism and audio-visual spectacle that with each new film finds "startling new ways to combine the vocabulary of exploitation cinema with often progressive but always subversive social and cultural forms" (Hassler-Forest, 2017, p. 306). The 1979 release of the first *Mad Max* film also coincided with the beginnings of deinstitutionalisation in Australia and, as such, the representation of intellectual disability in this film reflects social unease regarding how to meaningfully support this group within the community. The United Nations published two documents that informed much of the civil rights movements around deinstitutionalism at the time—the 1971 United Nations Declaration on the Rights of Mentally Retarded Persons and the 1975 Declaration on the Rights of Disabled Persons (Wiesel & Bigby, 2015). Both documents embraced an ethos of normalisation which replicated the conditions of everyday life for people with intellectual disability being as close as possible to those without. Australia was a signatory to the latter. In an apocalypse, the most vulnerable perish and are unlikely to be supported in post-apocalyptic dystopian futures. With people having intellectual disability only recently being afforded a place in 1970s Australia, *Mad Max* and *Mad Max: Beyond Thunderdome* exhibit concern for where this group will fit in a post-apocalyptic world devoid of any formal social support structure. This has resulted in a contradictory characterisation whereby intellectually disabled characters (Benno and Blaster) are included but feared, reminiscent of "not in my backyard" campaigns initiated during periods of deinstitutionalisation.

When Max, Jessie and Sprog flee from the bikers in *Mad Max* to the safety of Aunt May's remote property, Benno, an intellectually disabled minor character, is introduced. May, who wears calipers on her legs, warns Jessie not to be worried if she meets Benno down at the beach since he's "only a baby". As Jessie is chased through the bush by Toecutter's gang, her terror is intensified when she also encounters a toothless Benno who is not a baby, rather a very large intellectually disabled man unable to communicate with her. However, both Aunt May and Benno are portrayed as resilient and self-sufficient. Aunt May, an ageing disabled woman in a caring role, takes on Toecutter and his gang in an attempt to protect Jessie and Sprog, at first shooting at them and locking them in a building—an act that would have allowed Max's family to get away if their car had not overheated. May is the only woman in the film in a position of authority, setting the template for female leadership in the following films (see Chap. 4).

Significantly, the main protagonist in *Fury Road* is a disabled woman. Furiosa, played by Charlize Theron, challenges the gendered norms of action cinema (see Chap. 4). Likewise, her disability extends cinematic possibilities available to people with impairment. Yet this aspect has received only limited attention in both the popular reviews and academic explorations of gender and of *Fury Road*. Furiosa *is* the Interceptor as her amputated arm merges with machines to render her the superior road warrior. Like Max she has booby-trapped her vehicle so others can't drive it, but unlike Max the car will not explode, it simply will not drive unless the kill switch combination is employed.

Furiosa drives and shoots with more accuracy than road warrior Max. Like Max at the end of *Mad Max* driving through the wasteland in an almost dream-like state, Furiosa drives through a sandstorm displaying a mastery over her vehicle and protecting her precious cargo. The camera is trained on her face which has a look of determination. Ironically, at the same time Nux, with Max as his blood bag attached to the front of his vehicle, is on a—what turns out to be failed—kamikaze mission. In another key scene in *Fury Road*, Max is unable to hit his target and, with only one bullet left, wordlessly passes the gun to Furiosa and lowers his shoulder for her to use for support to ultimately make the successful shot (see Fig. 3.1). Theron comments on the uniqueness of the role:

Fig. 3.1 Max wordlessly drops his shoulder to offer Furiosa support to shoot at The Bullet Farmer in *Fury Road*. She makes the shot, blinding him

> I relished the idea of playing an amputee and hero. I was like, this is not going to come around anytime again. In the ultimate hardcore action film they're going to make the female lead be an amputee? This is ... great. (Rosen, 2015)

Whereas Max is a loner and nomad, Furiosa's leadership style could be described as interdependent. She values and recognises the abilities of each member of her group and within herself (see Chap. 4). While becoming an Imperator affords her power within the context of Immortan Joe's world, she uses that power to free his wives so that they can raise their children in safety.

Although a despot, Immortan Joe does not exclude people from powerful positions because of disability or impairment. For example, the differing abilities of the War Boys, many of whom are sickly, blind or weak, are acknowledged and they are given different roles in combat. Fletcher and Primack (2017) locate this inclusivity as a critique of compulsory able-bodiedness, claiming that "from Immortan Joe's political leadership to the instances of difference within the War Boys, many aspects of Immortan Joe's society demonstrate that norms related to ability are no longer considered when evaluating the worth of individuals" (p. 350). This approach is likewise evident in the earlier films as disabled characters contribute to their communities.

The Road Warrior is deeply concerned with the idea of contribution to society and the importance of human connection. In the film Max has become the terminal crazy he feared becoming in *Mad Max* and spends his time scavenging the post-apocalyptic desert wasteland. He comes upon an oil rich community of survivors and agrees to join them for a time to help them escape a menacing group of outlaws in exchange for the return of his car. In addition to Max's own impairment, the group's leader Pappagallo walks with a limp and the highly skilled mechanic's legs are completely paralysed—he uses a hoist for mobility (see Fig. 3.2). The Feral Kid is mute throughout the film but voices the concluding voiceover revealing that he eventually becomes a new world leader.

Beyond Thunderdome continues the theme of social contribution, with Max again beginning the film as a nomad, this time looking far removed from any civilising influence with his long hair and dusty appearance. It does not appear that he is wearing the leg brace from *The Road Warrior*, yet later when he meets the Lost Tribe of children he has a bandaged knee. When he tries to gain entry to Bartertown he is at first denied but his quick reflexes, hyper-vigilance and mastery of weaponry gain him entry. As he is led to Aunty Entity's inner sanctum, he passes TonTon, a blind saxophonist playing a beautiful song. In Greek mythology blindness is invoked in the context of both punishment and musical ability. Perhaps the musician was blinded as punishment for failing one of Entity's tests or it is possible this musician was blinded during the apocalypse (see Chap. 5 for a discussion of Miller's use of mythology). Entity instructs him to "play something tragic" as she appraises Max and recounts her own story:

Fig. 3.2 Max first appears in *The Road Warrior* a "shell of a man" with a full leg brace

> Do you know who I was? Nobody. Except on the day after, I was still alive. This nobody had a chance to be somebody.

Aunty Entity was developed to be both a villain and a hero, or perhaps as someone who was once a hero but had become a villain. Drawing on Joseph Campbell's myth theory, George Miller explains the origins of Aunty Entity:

> We didn't want to fall into a kind of fairly clichéed bad guy. And we have a saying that today's tyrant is yesterday's hero. And if you really look at the rhythm of the way things are, that's often the case. You have political heroes, for instance ... but if you go back to the classical sense, the definition of a hero, as far as we can decide, is that they're the agents of evolution. They are the characters by which the world changes to a new order, usually for the better. (Miller as cited in Billson, 2015)

This aesthetic is continued into *Fury Road* and forms a significant aspect of Max's characterisation. At the end of each film he has an opportunity to remain with civilisation—as symbolised by the small communities he encounters—but instead continues his nomad existence. Power breeds corruption and for Max to continue as a vehicle of social critique he must continue his perpetual journey.

Although Aunty Entity rules Bartertown with an iron fist, she is unable to dominate the disabled duo Master Blaster. For Max, however, the duo appears comical: "a big guy giving a little guy a piggy back". However, Aunty Entity and her entourage seem to fear them as very powerful. Indeed, Master is the only one who knows how to operate all the machinery that keeps Bartertown running, so he controls the means of production with Blaster providing protection. Aunty Entity, in an attempt to regain power over Master, manipulates Max into challenging Blaster to a gladiatorial battle in the Thunderdome. However, when Max defeats Blaster in battle he is unable to kill him because, upon knocking off his helmet, he realises Blaster has Down syndrome. In this scene another connection is made to the first film when the intellectually disabled Benno is described as just a baby by Aunt May. Max's refusal to kill Blaster suggests a degree of redemption or a return to valuing human life that he lost upon losing his family in the initial film (see Barbour, 1999); when this happens the master of ceremonies speaks to the crowd, saying that "look at us now, busted up and everyone talking about hard rain", implying a collective impairment and that all are subjected to fallout. The scene at once invokes and erases disability because there does not appear to be anyone with an impairment in the crowd except for Master.

A concern with societal contribution culminates in *Fury Road* as a significant number of main characters exhibit physical or emotional impairment because of a traumatic event. Max himself has PTSD, Furiosa has an amputated arm, Nux and the War Boys have a blood-based cancer, possibly leukaemia, and Immortan Joe's body is pitted with scars and trauma and he uses a breathing apparatus. Several of the guardians of the elevator platform who are tasked with selecting children of the citadel to become War Boys also use breathing apparatus. Even Immortan Joe's sons are a hyperbolised version of Master Blaster—Corpus Colossus, like Master, has the brains and control over the citadel, while his brother Rictus Erectus has the muscle like Blaster but also appears cognitively impaired, and each wear naso-oxygen tubes.

Other minor characters with disability feature throughout the so-called Wretched, the population of the citadel. As Immortan Joe is helped up in his apparatus to speak to a chanting crowd outside we see one of his helpers, a large bald man, also wearing an oxygen tank with tubes into his nose. Behind and to the left is a smaller bald man with a beard laying back in a chair. The next cut shows a crowd looking up towards Immortan Joe—the first image is of a man with a severed hand covered by a metallic cup holding a tin pan chanting along with the others. In medium close-up as Joe speaks to the crowd, he is assisted by another bald man with tubes in his nose and a surgical elasticised mask on his lower face who holds the microphone for Joe to speak. This is an iconic scene that draws on several sword and sandal spectacles from the 1950s. Another scene combines visual imagery in both *Freaks* and *Metropolis*, as the dehydrated Wretched rush towards the descending cascading water that Joe has released, the camera tracks right and we see in the foreground a legless man climbing over the rocks towards the water.

Whereas in the majority of cinematic representation disability and trauma are typically culturally encoded as an individual's personal tragedy, all of the characters throughout the *Mad Max* series have experienced trauma, loss and/or the effects of impairment. That is, in the post-apocalypse, trauma, loss and disablement is the norm—these experiences are recognised as collective and are attributed to whoever or whatever destroyed the world. For example, as Max attempts to disconnect from the community he has found refuge with in *The Road Warrior*, Pappagallo calls him a scavenger and implores him to tell his story of what burnt him out:

> Lose some family? Oh, so that's it. You lost some family. That make you something special, does it? Listen to me. Do you think you're the only one that's suffered? We've all been through it in here, but we haven't given up. We're still human beings with dignity. But you, you're out there with the garbage.

With his community ties Pappagallo hasn't given up on hope or leadership, whereas Max the nomad has. This concept of a pointless existence is revisited in *Beyond Thunderdome* when Max shatters the hope of the Lost Tribe of children by declaring that he is not their anticipated saviour Captain Walker and that the world they imagine is gone, saying "it's worse than nothing". This type of resignation is conveyed again when the Pig Killer is unconcerned that he's received a life sentence because "Down here life's two, three years". Likewise, in *Fury Road*, when Furiosa tells Splendid that "everything out here hurts" she emphasises that it is probably better to be dead than alive, regardless of whether one has a disability.

Desirable Skills: Disabled Mechanics

Significantly, road warrior Max encounters a number of disabled mechanics during his wanderings. Each one performs a key role in Max's survival and how and why he becomes who he is. There is Barry, the Main Force Patrol (MFP) mechanic who stutters uncontrollably in *Mad Max*, the aptly named The Mechanic with paralysed legs in *The Road Warrior*, Blackfinger who has a brace on his hand in *Beyond Thunderdome,* and the terminally-ill War Boys in *Fury Road*. Each character has desirable skills, an affinity with Max, and an important role in rebuilding the world.

Although a significant amount of popular and scholarly attention has been given to Max's traumatic response to losing his wife and child in the first film, the most genuine human emotion from Max in this film is when he first sees the V8 Interceptor, the car that his commanding officer Fifi hopes will seduce him into remaining with the MFP. Barry describes putting the car together with a "p p piece from here, a p p piece from there". Stuttering in cinema is typically employed as a humorous device or to denote anxiety, weakness or heroism or villainy (Johnson, 2008). Perhaps this stereotype is being invoked in *Mad Max* because Barry is nervous Max

Fig. 3.3 *The Road Warrior*'s Mechanic uses a hoist for mobility

will discover he's working for Fifi, attempting to manipulate him into staying with the MFP. At the same time, this character has an integral, perhaps heroic, role in the film—by joining Max and the Interceptor he creates the road warrior. Max begins the next film, *The Road Warrior,* a "shell of a man" with a full leg brace (see Fig. 3.3)—a reference to both Goose's full leg cast symbolic of impotence and Aunt May's calipers which conversely symbolise resilience in the first *Mad Max* film. Made from the hinges of a truck tailgate, Max's brace continues the "piece from here, piece from there" motor aesthetic introduced by Barry, the mechanic in *Mad Max,* and then revised in *Fury Road* with Furiosa's big rig acting as a kind of arm extension prosthetic.

Max's new pursuit car, the V8 Interceptor, is a symbol of both life and death. It lures Max back to the MFP, a decision that possibly caused him to lose his best mate, wife and child. Then it becomes his tool to avenge their deaths and later his mobile home. The mechanic in *The Road Warrior* uses a hoist and sling for mobility throughout the film. However, that disability does not prevent him from finding Max's booby-trap to blow up the car. Perhaps the character was, like Barry, an MFP mechanic because he recognises Max's car as "the last of the V8 Interceptors", a piece of history. The character restores both Max and the Interceptor, at one point he even oils Max's knee.

The third film, *Beyond Thunderdome,* features Blackfinger, a skilled, disabled mechanic whose hand is enclosed in a mechanical frame, at once aligning him with machinery and with Max who at this point in the franchise has been established as cyborg-like. Unlike *The Road Warrior*'s mechanic, Blackfinger is not able to disarm Max's booby-trapped car, suggesting further entropy and decline—civilisation, and the MFP, is long gone. This failure to disarm the car gives Max an opportunity to capture Master Blaster's attention. Although the film again concludes with Max returning to his nomad existence, Aunty Entity envisions a role for Blackfinger in rebuilding Bartertown, although Blackfinger appears to be the only member of Aunty Entity's army that does not want to help rebuild it. Nevertheless, their final, although brief, exchange suggests the continued significance of a disabled character as essential in rebuilding the post-apocalyptic world.

While, up to this point, the original trilogy presents lone disabled mechanics with integral roles in Max's survival, *Fury Road* features a paramilitary cult army of mechanics called the War Boys. The War Boys are offered up to Immortan Joe by their parents, the Wretched, who live in the citadel. Only the most able and healthy get selected (see origin story in Miller, Sexton, Lathouris, Jones, & Burchielli, 2015); and they are taught to worship and learn everything about mechanics and weaponry. However, as they become more deeply indoctrinated into the cult of the V8 and are further exposed to engine fumes, they acquire blood-borne cancers which require transfusions from donors such as Max. *Fury Road* also features an "organic mechanic", a cynical paramedic with no empathy. He is more familiar with Immortan Joe than anyone else in the film, referring to him variously as Joe or boss. His crucial, highly specialised competence—being responsible for the medical procedures carried out in the citadel—affords him this familiarity.

Conclusion

This chapter argues that disability dominates the world of *Mad Max*. Indeed, a significant number of disabled characters appear throughout the four films, and many operate as highly skilled members of various communities attempting to rebuild the world. Miller is clear about his motivations for *Mad Max*—road trauma, disablement and damaging social practices. While disability is at times used as a metaphor or as cinematic shorthand, the four films offer a variety of social critiques reflective of the social anxieties of the time, including deinstitutionalisation, social contribution and gender restrictions.

This chapter drew on Tobin Siebers' observation that the ideology of ability mandates that ability becomes the defining characteristic of humans while disability is individualised as a random event, something not common to all humans. Each *Mad Max* film critiques this ideology in various ways, for example, via Aunt May's resilience in the first film; the contributions of the mechanics throughout all films; and via both Max and Furiosa's leadership as road warriors. *Fury Road* in particular critiques the ideology of ability discussed throughout this chapter and opens a cinematic space for disability inclusion. With its disabled protagonists, antagonists and minor characters, *Fury Road* uses the post-apocalyptic discourse to reimagine society without any sort of social support. The next chapter moves on to an in-depth analysis of gender in *Fury Road* as an epistemological lens through which to view the preceding films.

References

Barbour, D. H. (1999). Heroism and redemption in the *Mad Max* trilogy. *Journal of Popular Film and Television, 27*(3), 28–34. https://doi.org/10.1080/01956059909602806

Berger, J. (2004). Trauma without disability, disability without trauma: A disciplinary divide. *JAC, 24*(3), 563–582.

Billson, A. (2015). George Miller talks about *Mad Max*, heroes & Tina Turner: The 1985 interview. Retrieved from https://multiglom.com/2015/05/12/george-miller-the-1985-interview/

Blowen, M. (1985). *Mad Max* creator has a point to make. *Boston Globe* (p. 29). Boston, MA.

Bogdan, R. (2012). *Picturing disability: Beggar, freak, citizen and other photographic rhetoric*. Syracuse, NY: Syracuse University Press.

Casper, M. J., & Morrison, D. R. (2012). Intersections of disability studies and critical trauma studies: A provocation. *Disability Studies Quarterly, 32*(2). https://doi.org/10.18061/dsq.v32i2.3189

Finkelstein, V. (1980). Attitudes and disabled people: Issues for discussion. *Disability Archive UK*. Retrieved from http://www.leeds.ac.uk/disability-studies/archiveuk/finkelstein/attitudes.pdf

Fletcher, B., & Primack, A. J. (2017). Driving toward disability rhetorics: Narrative, crip theory, and eco-ability in *Mad Max: Fury Road*. *Critical Studies in Media Communication, 34*(4), 344–357. https://doi.org/10.1080/15295036.2017.1329540

Gagnon, J. M. (2016). Lessons in suffering: Greek tragedy's teachings on disability through Sophocles' Philoctetes. *New Political Science, 38*(3), 335–353. https://doi.org/10.1080/07393148.2016.1189029

Garland-Thomson, R. (1997). *Extraordinary bodies: Figuring physical disability in American culture and literature*. New York, NY: Columbia University Press.

Garland-Thomson, R. (2015, April 30). Eugenic world building and the problem of disability. *RN Big Ideas*. Retrieved from http://www.abc.net.au/radionational/programs/bigideas/disability-and-bioethics/6427260

Hassler-Forest, D. (2017). *Mad Max:* Between apocalypse and utopia. *Science Fiction Film and Television, 10*(3), 301–443. https://doi.org/10.3828/sfftv.2017.21

Johnson, J. K. (2008). The visualization of the twisted tongue: Portrayals of stuttering in film, television, and comic books. *Journal of Popular Culture, 41*(2), 245–261. https://doi.org/10.1111/j.1540-5931.2008.00501.x

Kumari Campbell, F. (2009). *Contours of ableism: The production of disability and abledness*. New York, NY: Palgrave Macmillan.

Kuppers, P. (2008). Encountering paralysis: Disability, trauma and narrative. In E. A. Kaplan & B. Wang (Eds.), *Trauma and cinema: Cross-cultural explorations*. Aberdeen & Hong Kong: Hong Kong University Press.

Longmore, P. (1987). Screening stereotypes: Images of disabled people in television and motion pictures. In A. Gartner & T. Joe (Eds.), *Images of the disabled, disabling images* (pp. 65–78). New York, NY: Praeger.

Mathews, S. (1984). *35mm dreams*. Ringwood, VIC: Penguin.

McRuer, R. (2006). *Crip theory: Cultural signs of queerness and disability*. New York, NY; London, UK: New York University Press.

Miller, G., Sexton, M., Lathouris, N., Jones, T., & Burchielli, R. (2015). A prelude to the blockbuster film *Mad Max: Fury Road*. DC Comics.

O'Regan, T. (2005). *Australian national cinema*. London, UK; New York, NY: Routledge.

Quayson, A. (2007). *Aesthetic nervousness: Disability and the crisis of representation*. New York, NY: Columbia University Press.

Rodriguez, R. (2015). Interview: Director George Miller on *Mad Max: Fury Road*. Retrieved from https://www.star-telegram.com/entertainment/arts-culture/article20797569.html

Rosen, L. (2015, November 19). The plan was for Furiosa to be an amputee, and Charlize Theron made sure they stuck to the plan. *LA Times*. Retrieved from http://www.latimes.com/entertainment/envelope/la-en-charlize-theron-20151119-story.html

Siebers, T. (2010). *Disability aesthetics*. Ann Arbor, MI: University of Michigan Press.

Siebers, T. (2013). Disability and the theory of complex embodiment – For identity politics in a new register. In L. Davis (Ed.), *The disability studies reader* (4th ed., pp. 278–296). Hoboken, NJ: Routledge.

Traverso, A., & Broderick, M. (2010). Interrogating trauma: Towards a critical trauma studies. *Continuum, 24*(1), 3–15. https://doi.org/10.1080/10304310903461270

Wiesel, I., & Bigby, C. (2015). Movement on shifting sands: Deinstitutionalisation and people with intellectual disability in Australia, 1974–2014. *Urban Policy and Research, 33*(2), 1–17. https://doi.org/10.1080/08111146.2014.980902

CHAPTER 4

Gender

Abstract From the initial film to *Fury Road,* the *Mad Max* series consciously plays with notions and representations of gendered sexuality, problematising conventions of masculinity and femininity, patriarchy and feminism; examples of characters include the Warrior Woman of *Mad Max 2*, the matriarch Aunty Entity in *Beyond Thunderdome* and the hero Furiosa in *Fury Road.* Similarly, masculinity is problematised by Max himself across the four films as well as by Johnny the Boy in *Mad Max* and Immortan Joe and the War Boys in *Fury Road.* This chapter draws on these characters as well as gender, disability, trauma and monster theory to examine the franchise's gendered evolution over its near four decades of existence.

Keywords Gender • Disability • Post-feminism • Monster theory • Masculinity

The leather-clad image of Mel Gibson as Mad Max along with his nitro-guzzling V8 Interceptor became the icon of Australian masculinity in the 1980s. The normative hero of Australia cinema of this period was typically male and in charge—"physically strong, rugged, with chiselled features that suggest experience of the world and a manner that warns 'Don't mess with me'" (Enker, 1994, p. 281). They are Rosemarie Garland-Thomson's normate (Garland-Thomson, 1997). Yet, while Max's character was

M. Broderick, K. Ellis, *Trauma and Disability in Mad Max*,
https://doi.org/10.1007/978-3-030-19439-0_4

initially conceived as a conduit through which to reflect on the damaging effects of this brand of masculinity, it would go on to spawn a whole new generation of the "last man standing" archetype.

The introductory voiceover to the second film in the series, *The Road Warrior*, recounts the apocalypse as having been set off by economic collapse and civil war, blaming world leaders—men—who:

> talked and talked and talked, but nothing could stem the avalanche, their world crumbled, cities exploded, a whirlwind of looting, a firestorm of fear, men began to feed on men.

At the time *The Road Warrior* was made, filmic action heroes did not tend to "talk", neither did Max. This image of the silent, vengeful hero had a lasting impact on political leaders at the time and became a staple of action cinema. In reference to what to do in the case of future hostage crises, Ronald Reagan is quoted as saying "Boy, after seeing 'Rambo' last night, I know what to do the next time this happens" (Times Staff Writer, 1985).

However, in the latest instalment of the *Mad Max* franchise, *Fury Road*, a group of women, some pregnant, others ageing, are instead being led from captivity not by the typical silent male hero but by a disabled woman. With the initial chase set in motion by five wives (so-called breeders) who are considered the property ("stuff" according to one War Boy) of their captor Immortan Joe, George Miller knew a man was not up to the task of escaping Joe's compound: "they needed a road warrior to escort the wives, it couldn't be a male because that's a different story, the man stealing five wives of a tyrant. She had to be female, she had to be an experienced road warrior" (MacInnes, 2015).

Enter Furiosa. Female. Disabled. Road warrior.

The central question critics pose in regard to *Fury Road* is therefore gender, and the film has been both widely celebrated and criticised for its feminist message. Feminist author and blogger Jessica Valenti praises the film as forward thinking for depicting "the horror of sexism and the necessity of freedom from patriarchy" (Valenti, 2015). However, men's rights' activists took less favourably to the gendered interactions between Max and Furiosa in the film, believing Max had become a secondary character in his own franchise due to a pervasive feminist agenda overtaking Hollywood. In his call to boycott *Fury Road*, *Return of the Kings* columnist Aaron Clarey displayed an astonishing lack of insight to the national and gendered dynamics of the franchise when he declared "Nobody barks orders to Mad Max" claiming the latest instalment ruined and rewrote "a piece of American culture" (Clarey, 2015). But what has gone less remarked, or only mentioned obliquely, is the way *Fury Road*'s contemplation on gender also interrogates masculinity and the symbolic roles disability and trauma play in this interrogation.

From *Mad Max* to *Fury Road,* the Australian series consciously foregrounds notions and representations of gendered sexuality, problematising conventions of masculinity and femininity, patriarchy and feminism. Examples of such characters include the ageing and disabled Aunt May in *Mad Max*, the Warrior Woman from *The Road Warrior*, Savannah Nix, the new world mother of post-nuke Sydney and the matriarch Aunty Entity in *Beyond Thunderdome,* and the hero Imperitor Furiosa in *Fury Road*. Similarly, masculinity is problematised by Max himself across the four films as well as by Johnny the Boy in *Mad Max* and Immortan Joe and the War Boys in *Fury Road*. This chapter draws on these characters as well as gender, disability, trauma and monster theory to examine the franchise's evolution over its four decades of existence.

Fury Road was released in 2015, coincidently, the same year that marked the 40th anniversary of Laura Mulvey's influential essay *Visual Pleasure and Narrative Cinema* in which Mulvey observes men act and women are acted upon in classical Hollywood film. That is, women's presence in film narrative is solely for the feelings and emotions she can incite in the male (Mulvey, 1975). For example, Max's wife Jessie performs this function in the first film. The attack on Jessie ultimately prompts Max to embrace the chaos and lawless existence he has admitted to fearing but also enjoying. His revenge narrative takes a tumultuous ride, beginning in *Mad Max*, continuing throughout *The Road Warrior* and *Beyond Thunderdome* and culminating in a chaos narrative of near redemption in *Fury Road*. Miller's films also display what Mulvey foregrounded as fetishistic scopophilia and sadistic voyeurism, where men in these movies—and we as the audience—view acts of sex and violence often via a narratological controlling gaze (Mulvey, 1975).

Gender and Sexuality

Despite the intensely feminist message of *Fury Road* and the unpacking of gender constructions throughout the other three films, the films that make up the *Mad Max* series do, however, perpetuate some problematic imagery related to gender and sexuality. Firstly, *Mad Max* and *The Road Warrior* invoke imagery of homosexual bikers to represent danger and a threat to Max's body. Miller has noted that in the first two films he:

> wanted to avoid the cliché of the modern day biker gang that you saw in Roger Corman movies of the sixties, with the biker and his old lady. To have homosexuality amongst some of the members of the gang played off that cliché. (Miller as cited in Mathews, 1984, p. 242)

Their presence works in the first two films to symbolise the coming of the apocalypse and death. Symbolically, Max's body is under threat. Citing the *Mad Max* films among other examples (e.g. the films of Clint Eastwood and Charlton Heston) Steve Neale suggests "male" genres and films involve "narcissistic phantasies of power, omnipotence, mastery and control" (Neale, 1982, p. 5). For Neale, heterosexual masculinity has been problematically identified as a normative structure, both in relation to images of men and women, whereas male homosexuality is something mainstream cinema "assiduously seeks either to denigrate or deny" (p. 15). The opening sequence to *Mad Max,* where Max slowly and methodically prepares to enter the chase with the Nightrider, signifies his position as the narrative's dominant male—this characterisation continues throughout the first three films and arguably into *Fury Road*. In comparison, the other police officers are framed as unfocused, out of control and unreliable. While Goose impulsively enters the chase and injures his leg, thus later requiring a full leg cast, Max, however, is in complete control. In addition to these hasty hyper-masculine but ultimately vulnerable characters, Max is established in direct comparison to the feminine figures in the film, including his wife Jessie who exists exclusively in the domestic sphere; his queer superior officer Fifi who lovingly tends to his indoor plants topless and in tight leather pants while imploring Max the world needs heroes, even offering to get on his knees to beg him to stay; and the homoerotic undertones of Toecutter's gang of bikers.

As discussed in the previous chapter, Tom O'Regan observes an anxiety about physical threat to the male body throughout *Mad Max* (O'Regan, 2005). This is evident in the minor and major injuries acquired by the Main Force Patrol (MFP). While noting that audience identification in cinema involves many forms of desire, and is always multiple, fluid and sometime contradictory, Neale nevertheless suggests that "patriarchal images of masculinity" constantly involve "sado-masochistic themes" where men, as heroes, are occasionally "marked as the object of an erotic gaze" (Neale, 1982, p. 9). In this context imagery of damaged men's bodies in heteronormative, mainstream cinema serves to deflect sexualised identification. Several characters experience disabling effects of road trauma throughout the first *Mad Max*. Charlie, in Big Bopper's car, after a hot pursuit chasing the Nightrider and his moll, Marmaduke, ends up partly impaled on the dashboard with his throat stuck on some glass from the windscreen. Later, inside the halls of justice, Max awaits Goose who rides a motorbike with his entire right leg in a cast. When Goose is later burnt alive by Toecutter's gang, Max is unable to come to terms with the complete disfigurement of his partner and resigns from the MFP fearing he will become like the outlaws—he's already enjoying it too much. In mainstream patriarchal cinema, mutilation and sadism are often the signs of both repression and the means by which the male body may be "disqualified" as an "object of erotic contemplation and desire" (Neale, 1982, p. 8). Max undertakes a road trip with Jessie and Sprog; however, it is on this trip that Toecutter and his gang can enact their brutal revenge on Max for killing the Nightrider. As the bikers terrorise Jessie, she accidently dismembers Cundalini's hand and the bikers now directly target Jessie and kidnap Sprog.

Women and children are unsafe in this environment. Early scenes where they are run off the road or abused by menacing men foreshadow Jessie and Sprog's deaths. Later in the film after a woman is raped, the perpetrators are released because witnesses are too frightened to testify in court. Even Fifi, the chief of MFP, is unsympathetic, describing the raped woman to Max and Goose as "the town bike". Yet the issue here is the men's bodies, the danger these bikers could wreak on the masculine heterosexual body rather than the damage they're already wreaked on an unnamed female. Indeed, Australian cinema has been consistently criticised for including female rape as a way to strength masculine bonds (Heller-Nicholas, 2012).

The theme of rape, captivity and sexual assault continued during pre-production on *Fury Road*. Miller employed Eve Ensler (author of *The Vagina Monologues*) as a consultant to help impart psycho-cultural "depth" to the female cast, especially in relation to gendered trauma and recovery, though it is debatable whether this translated into effective characterisation within the film. According to Rosie Huntington-Whiteley, the actor who plays Splendid (the pregnant wife of Immortan Joe), Ensler worked with the principal female actors to help them craft their roles to be more than "just five beautiful girls". She did this by relaying tragic stories from her experience of working with both rape victims in the Congo and with other women "who have had unthinkable things happen to them through the power of men's hands" (Ensler, as cited in Baxter, 2017).

Ensler's input was seen as important to the development of the female characters—implicit in *Fury Road*'s presentation of these women is that they are sex slaves, held captive as "breeders" for Immortan Joe and his male, genetically damaged progeny. Yet, as Angela Watercutter notes, dialogue in *Fury Road* is scarce, perhaps as pared back and perfunctory as in the first two films, and the women are never directly referred to as prisoners. For Watercutter this is accomplished by Miller's ability to "show rather than tell":

> No one *says* the women in Joe's dominion are sex slaves—they are just shown pregnant or being hooked up to milking machines or leaving hateful messages scrawled on the walls. (Watercutter, 2015)

Indeed, Immortan Joe's harem of young women is stylistically composed early on as pre-Raphaelite figures, who on occasion also resemble Botticelli damsels, until they use heavy bolt-cutters to remove their medieval, metal chastity belts, or spit obscene invective at both Max and Nux. Narrative discourse does, however, provide one rare insight into a character's backstory. Imperator Furiosa tersely explains to Max that the "Green Place" she seeks as a refuge for Immortan Joe's wives was the area where she was born, but also from which she was "taken as a child. Stolen".

These gendered visual and verbal invocations of abduction, slavery, assault and unspoken trauma permeate *Fury Road* as counterpoint to Max's internal soliloquies and hauntings. The overarching trauma inflicted upon both *homo sapiens*—and the entire planet—is implicitly male-generated. For consultant Ensler, director Miller "made a feminist action film" set in a post-holocaust future and informed by contemporary global concerns:

> One out of three women on the planet will be raped or beaten in her lifetime—it's a central issue of our time, and that violence against women relates to racial and economic injustice. This movie takes those issues head-on. (Ensler, as cited in Shaw-Williams, 2015)

Max

Max's response to trauma undergoes a significant shift across the four films and ascribes to changing social conceptions of masculinity. For example, in *Mad Max* he enters Goose's hospital room with rage and purpose but after seeing his partner's burnt body he flees, unable to articulate his feelings—"that's not The Goose". He later laments to his wife Jessie, that Goose was "so full of living" in almost disbelief that he was gone. Max does not share his grief beyond this. Then when Jessie is run down by the same gang, Max does not enter her hospital room, hovering outside near the door (see Fig. 4.1), ultimately fleeing civilised society to take revenge on Toecutter and Johnny the Boy.

Throughout *The Road Warrior* and *Beyond Thunderdome* Max does not connect with the communities he encounters on the level he did with Goose and Jessie. His rapport with the Feral Kid (in *The Road Warrior*) and the Lost Tribe of children (*Beyond Thunderdome*) is fleeting and superficial. In these films, Max is always out of frame when someone is injured or remains hyper-focused on his task, such as in *The Road Warrior* when the Warrior Woman is pierced in the stomach by Wez and falls from the top of the oil tanker. As the mechanic tries to pull her back on top of the tanker and Max turns to look, both the Warrior Woman and the mechanic fall under the wheels of the tanker. Max does not go back for them.

However, despite his reputation as an iconic image of generation X machismo, Max's masculinity is constantly called into question. In *The*

Fig. 4.1 Max cannot bring himself to enter Jessie's hospital room in *Mad Max*

Road Warrior Pappagallo rejects his offer to drive the tanker, saying, "Look at yourself Max; you couldn't even drive a wheelchair". Max's closed-over eye and limping body invoke impending doom as the group plan to escape the Humungus' gang. However, within the context of 1980s machismo, as mentioned earlier, Max's injuries can be read as a sadistic neutralisation of the eroticisation of Max as a male action hero, his injuries depicting a triumph of masculinity tested (see Neale, 1982).

In direct contrast to Cleary's aforementioned assertion that "nobody barks orders at Max" (Clarey, 2015), he receives direction from women throughout the series. For example, the Warrior Woman in *The Road Warrior,* Savanah Nix and Aunty Entity in *Beyond Thunderdome*. Aunty Entity demands that he challenge Blaster in the Thunderdome, casts him into the desert for busting a deal and belittles Max by calling him "a raggedyman" at key points in *Beyond Thunderdome*. However, in *Fury Road,* Max begins to re-connect with women and process his historical injuries and trauma, a key aspect of recovery narratives (Gumb, 2018). For example, despite being engaged in battle with the People Eater, he returns to the war rig when The Dag calls to him that Furiosa is hurt "real bad" when she, like the Warrior Woman of *The Road Warrior,* is pierced by an arrow in the stomach. Earlier he had refused to turn back for Splendid when she went under the wheels. While the Max in *Mad Max* is unable to deal with traumatic injury and disablement, and in *The Road Warrior* and *Beyond Thunderdome* either does not acknowledge its presence or uses it for his own gain—for example, trading Nathan for entry into Pappagallo's compound then demanding the community honour the deal the dying man had made—*Fury Road*'s Max recognises the importance of collaboration and interdependence.

As Furiosa lies dying, the Vuvalini invoke a rhetoric of body autonomy as they describe her injuries: "She's pumping air into her chest cavity. She's collapsing her lungs ... one breath at a time". In this moment of near-death Max finally tells her his name. Critics have largely interpreted this as Max convincing himself of who he is:

> Having disremembered himself for so long, he re-remembers and reclaims himself again in his mirroring communion with Furiosa. It is simultaneously the moment of self-discovery and self-revelation. (Du Plooy, 2018, p. 11)

In this moment of trauma Max again moves closer to the self he lost when his wife lay dying in the same way: “Multiple traumas, spleen, liver, lung, flail chest, left neck of femur, renal shutdown”.

The notion of loss or of processing loss is a site at which disability and trauma studies could merge. As James Berger explains:

> A theory of disability might well try to include a theory of loss specific to disability—that is, the loss of physical, mental, and neurological capacities. The world itself, and one’s own body, must be relearned, processes clearly analogous to some of the central concerns of trauma studies. One would think that a theory of disability would address such questions of trauma, loss, mourning, and regeneration that seem so closely associated with many people’s experiences of disability. (Berger, 2004, p. 572)

Max has had to re-learn his body, his mind and the world around him as it further disintegrates. His comments to Furiosa that “hope is a mistake” suggest he cannot look to the future, he exists only in the present with haunting intrusions from the past. This chaos narrative, as defined by Arthur Frank, “imagines life never getting better”, that is, they are anxiety provoking and offer little cultural reassurance (Frank, 1995). For example, with her focus on redemption, Furiosa is also unable to look beyond the past or the here and now. Indeed, Max and Furiosa have an extended conversation about hope and redemption across the course of the film. Furiosa describes the breeders as looking for hope while she is on a quest for redemption. The breeders are unique in this regard—their focus extends beyond the here and now. They acknowledge the past—“who killed the world”—but are determined for a better future—“we are not things”, “our babies will not be warlords”, “no unnecessary killing”. Max is initially dismissive of the notion of hope, claiming “hope is a mistake, if you can’t fix what’s broken you’ll go insane”. He later comes to embrace the concept—but never for himself—by convincing the women to return to the citadel and take it for themselves.

In this way, Max is characterised by an ethos of “caring masculinity” as defined by Karla Elliott:

> the central features of caring masculinities are their rejection of domination and their integration of values of care, such as positive emotion, interdependence, and relationality, into masculine identities. (Elliott, 2016, p. 240)

For example, when Furiosa is hurt, Max embraces a value of care when he becomes a blood bag again, this time invoking Christ-like connotations of self-sacrifice by voluntarily giving his blood to Furiosa. In a display of positive emotion and a rejection of domination he apologises abjectly as he pierces her lung to help her to breathe. He apologises again when he finds a vein to begin the blood transfusion.

Furiosa

Donna Haraway's *Cyborg Manifesto,* published in the context of the Reagan era, posited the cyborg as a radical figure of feminist critique. She framed the cyborg as a potential boundary breaker between humans and animals, animal-humans and machines and the physical and non-physical. In her manifesto, Haraway notes a feminist rejection of science and technology and posits the cyborg as a fruitful point of analysis (Haraway, 1990). Similarly, critical disability studies has positioned technology within the medical model of disability (Oliver, 1978) and prosthesis and rehabilitation in particular as evidence of a cultural rhetoric of compulsory able-bodiedness. Following Haraway we suggest the cyborg as an important site of analysis, particularly with reference to Max and Furiosa's bodies as they merge with machines.

Whereas the cyborg invokes connotations of superhumanness in disability studies or of transcending disability (Siebers, 2008), the cyborg is also a point of transgression as articulated by Alison Kafer:

> The cyborg figure certainly holds much promise for disability politics; from its suspicion of essentialist identities to its insistence on coalition work to its interrogation of ideologies of wholeness, the cyborg offers productive insights for developing a feminist disability vision of the future. (Kafer, 2013)

The cyborg therefore questions able-bodiedness and able-mindedness as compulsory. Drawing on mythology—discussed in depth in the next chapter—many heroes, deities, monsters and tyrants had impairments; some compensated with prosthetics which became iconographic aspects of their identity. Both Max and Furiosa's cyborg-like prosthetics are motor vehicles. While militarism and patriarchal capitalism may have caused their trauma and impairments, their choice of prosthesis offers a radical reinterpretation. In the first three films Max's reliance on the Interceptor is cyborg-like, particularly because his leg is wounded and his arm crushed by Bubba Zanetti. Similarly, Furiosa merges her body with an oil tanker in a cyborg embodiment in *Fury Road.* As Furiosa's prosthesis connects with the truck the embodiment becomes reminiscent of hyper-masculine action figures mass-produced for children in the 1970s such as GI Joe's Mike Power Atomic Man, Ideal Toy's Jay J. Armes and even the Six Million Dollar Man. However, Furiosa's prosthetic is absent at four key moments throughout the film in a display of vulnerability, strength, power and fairness. This absence also signals a rejection of the binary able versus the disabled.

The first is when Max and Nux initially encounter the group. The wives are bathing and Furiosa's prosthetic is hanging from the truck. It is a moment of vulnerability for the breeders and for Furiosa. Max, closely followed by Nux, approaches the women with masculine confidence. Despite holding Max as his prisoner for the duration of the film thus far, Nux proceeds from the assumption that Max will partner with him and together they work in synchronicity to acquire both a gun and bullets as Max engages in hand-to-hand combat with Furiosa. Despite starting in a seemingly vulnerable position—being a female with one arm—Furiosa initially overpowers Max (see Fig. 4.2).

The second instance where Furiosa is without her prosthesis is when she reacts to the news that the Green Place is gone. She walks off alone into the desert, removes the prosthesis and howls in a guttural sound of grief. The voices of the many mothers can be heard in the scene as the camera stays trained on Furiosa's face. Miller describes his intentions for the scene:

Fig. 4.2 Furiosa overpowers Max in hand-to-hand combat in *Fury Road*

> When anybody receives really devastating news it gets a little fragmented … You're picking up enough of the story so you understand something bad has happened without giving an environmental report on the place, and it was played on her face. (Miller, as cited in Sharf, 2018)

From these moments of vulnerability and grief, Furiosa is next without her prosthesis in a moment of triumph—when she kills Immortan Joe. Unlike Furiosa, Immortan Joe cannot survive without his prosthesis. In order to kill him, Furiosa hooks her arm to his breathing apparatus and then tears it off and throws it into a wheel. It is fitting that Furiosa should kill Immortan Joe in this way, by removing his hyper-masculine parodic armour and her own cyborg identity with the same action. Finally, when Furiosa claims the citadel, she does not wear her prosthesis. It does not matter to the crowd who chant her name. Whereas Immortan Joe retained power through an illusion of masculinity and patriarchal prowess, Furiosa takes the citadel as who she really is—a disabled female.

The *Mad Max* of the 1970s and 1980s was often read as initiating a new era of masculinity. He is recognised as iconic of generation X machismo and a reaction to both second wave feminism and misogyny (Du Plooy, 2018). However, as the series progresses, women move from being acted upon to becoming the agents of action. Furiosa, by comparison, is not explicitly discussed as inciting a new era of femininity, rather her cultural cache is recognised in terms of critiquing the patriarchy. During the 1980s and 1990s female action heroes such as Sarah Connor of *The Terminator* films were powerful but often assumed the role of sidekick. Even Aunty Entity of *Beyond Thunderdome* is not in complete control, with Master Blaster overseeing the crucial energy production and whose embargoes could shut down Bartertown. However, in *Fury Road*, Furiosa is the main character, with Max closer to the sidekick. Hence, the film is a post-feminist celebration of collaborative teamwork, the notion that women in popular culture are most powerful when they work in teams (such as *Buffy the Vampire Slayer*). Furiosa and her team are even more powerful because most of her team survive with her to take control of the citadel.

Indeed, interdependence and collaboration are key features of *Fury Road*. The term interdependence conveys a sense of mutual reliance or reciprocity. Within disability studies, interdependence is recognised as a more empowering subjectivity than independence or autonomy. Susan Wendell questions our cultural obsession with independence and positions *inter*dependence as a more productive way forward:

> we have to change social values to recognize the value of depending on others and being depended upon. This would also reduce the fear and shame associated with dependency in old age—a condition most of us will reach. (Wendell, 1989)

Fury Road embraces this ethos—Furiosa, Max, the breeders, Nux and the Vuvalini value and rely on each other. Rather than men acting individually and narcissistically, responsibilities are delegated according to skills and ability—for example, the wives take inventory because they are not skilled in combat or knowledgeable about cars, while both Max and Nux are only allowed to drive the big rig once they prove they are reliable. The diversity of women appearing in this film is also of significance by extending the possibilities afforded to women:

> The film does not judge its heroines on age and beauty: together, all of these women give the lie to the notion that there is any proper way to be female on film. Supermodels and white-haired warriors with faces like withered fruit fight side-by-side under a leader whose beauty is in no way sexualized. Together, they are formidable. (Penny, 2015)

As discussed earlier in the chapter, Miller went to great lengths to craft the breeders, several of whom are portrayed by lingerie models, as more than just five beautiful girls by hiring Eve Ensler as a consultant. In contrast to this widening of available roles for women in action cinema, masculinity is represented here as sick, weak and traumatised. As we mentioned in Chap. 1, Miller describes Max as becoming a full monster at the end of *Mad Max*; however, by *Fury Road* the monsters are more hyperbolised as Max regains his humanity. Yet these figures also offer a space for cultural critique and work to represent social and cultural failures on a massive scale.

Monsters, Freaks and Metaphors

Margrit Shildrick defines monstrous bodies as "bodies that in their gross failure to approximate to corporeal norms are radically excluded" (Shildrick, 2002, p. 2). The corporeal norm or normate is the standard against which other bodies are measured:

> The strong, well-formed, non-disabled, masculine body is the benchmark and against this benchmark a woman is found wanting and a disabled person—man or woman—is weak and vulnerable. (Hughes, 2009, p. 400)

The medical model of disability positions disability and disfigurement as undesirable, typically in contrast to the normative or non-disabled body which is presented as aesthetically preferable and something to which the disabled body should aspire. Many films follow this rhetoric, particularly those in the science fiction or horror genre. Within these films, physical impairment has become a key, defining feature of monsters who in turn act as a chimera through which to process a fear of disablement. The "uncertain cultural body" of the monster commands "restore my fragmented body" (Cohen, 1996). These monsters carry with them several negative connotations and are usually described in critical disability studies as damaging representations. However, as vehicles for society's anxieties, monsters provoke sympathy and critique the societies that create them. For example, the filmic adaptations of both *Frankenstein* (1931) and *Dracula* (1931) were made during a social period concerned with eugenics and of continuing "racial and biological purity" (Smith, 2012). Textually, the monsters appear to threaten heterosexual coupling and the body (*Dracula*) or the mind (*Frankenstein*) itself. By eradicating their monsters, these films seem to reinforce the normative body and mind as species typical and human. At the same time, they also problematise these constructions and reveal eugenics is an inherently flawed concept:

> Apparently cautionary eugenic tales morph into musings on the mutability, vulnerability, and obstinate materiality of the body. Disability appears not as something fixed and pathological, but rather as a generative, reproductive, and unstable encounter between textual and social constructs, on the one hand, and the embodied self, on the other. (Smith, 2012)

Nevertheless, films that feature monsters can offer a productive way to allegorically explore the social and cultural origins of the extraordinary body. Approaching monsters and freaks in *Mad Max* as metaphors conveying cultural fears and anxieties also invites a reading which privileges a *critique* of the ideology of ability as opposed to a *fear* of disability (see Chap. 3). Granted, the monsters display a deep ambivalence about who should be considered as members of societies (Johnny the Boy) and in fact who should become community leaders (Humungus, Aunty Entity and Immortan Joe), yet the monstrous body in *Fury Road* invites an investigation of toxic masculinity and its correspondence with late capitalism. As such, the monster is a contradictory image invoking both anxiety and empathy.

As cultural metaphors, monsters appear in different guises across different historical periods. The image of the monster is not fixed across time and space. As Ismere Lada-Richards explains, monsters have little in common except for their perceived relation to what is considered "the norm" in any particular culture (Lada-Richards, 1998).

Monstrous images of vulnerable, traumatic and disabled bodies act as cultural signifiers upon which "any given culture will readily attach its own communal meanings to them, thereby transforming a floating signifier into a collective representation capable of invoking particular meanings"(Siebers, 2010, p. 115). As such, a clear relationship exists between the monster and the freak in the realm of entertainment. Rosemarie Garland-Thomson suggests the popularity of the freak show shifted monsters "into the category of curiosity" (Garland-Thomson, 1996) and the disabled body itself has also been central to the cultural construction of both monsters and freaks. While the freak draws on the image of the monster, it differs in that the freak is not completely othered, "freaks bring monsters in closer proximity to 'normal' observer" (Wright, 2013, p. 81).

Cultural images of both the monster and the freak come together in the body of Immortan Joe, *Fury Road*'s dictatorial antagonist. He first appears with his back to the camera, an image covered in welts and scars with a War Pup blowing powder onto it (see Fig. 4.3).

Immortan Joe wheezes as his sons dress him in hyper-masculinised armour—a costume described by Miller as self-conscious militaristic "pag-

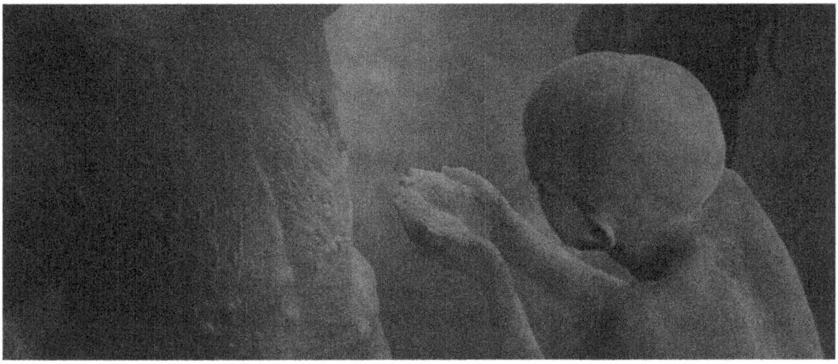

Fig. 4.3 A War Pup blows white powder onto Immortan Joe's back in *Fury Road*

moods, and makes the ethical decision to welcome Furiosa and the Wretched to the top of the citadel.

The War Boys and particularly Nux take the metaphor that patriarchy and product exploitation are making us all sick to the extreme. As Immortan Joe's "battle fodder", their goal in life is to die "glorious on the Fury Road". They make the quasi-religious sign of the V8 in an overt display of celebration of masculinity and embrace autocide. However, the V8 and their spray paint chroming rituals have added to their terminal illness. From a distance, the War Boys look strong and capable, albeit creepily white. However, when they appear in close range it is apparent their bodies are riddled with tumours. Death is their manifest destiny. When one War Boy does die on *Fury Road* he yells to the others to "witness" him, yet, after his death they insultingly describe it as "mediocre".

Nux comes to symbolise both hope and redemption in the film. Initially spurned by the breeders as Immortan Joe's battle fodder, and discarded by Max for previously imprisoning him, stealing his blood, jacket and car, Nux is alone and confused when the clear and dogmatic boundaries of his world begin to deconstruct. Life is short for the War Boys who are also described as being in their half-life; indoctrinated into believing that their purpose in life is to die in service of Immortan Joe. A quote attributed to Miller on the *Mad Max* wiki and fan site outlines the ways these characters are disabled within their social context:

> These War Boys have no choice. They're culturally impoverished: There's no books, there's no internet, there's no theaters, no radios, no music. All they have are the detritus of the past and they refashion it so a steering wheel becomes a religious artifact; they do the sign of the V8; the engine they scarified on their bodies, because an engine is much more permanent than the human body; they chrome their teeth, because chrome is such a rare thing. So like all cults this is another cult invented by the Immortan Joe in order to get people to die on his behalf. (Mad Max Wiki, n.d.)

While Nux is loyal to Immortan Joe throughout a significant period of the film, as he witnesses Immortan Joe watching Max driving the truck that kills Splendid (Joe's favourite wife), Nux refocuses his allegiance to Max, Furiosa and the breeders. Nux describes Max's plan to take the citadel as feeling "like hope". He plays an integral role in the plan, initially to act as a double agent "returning" the wives, but sacrifices himself in an ultimate act of heroism (see Chap. 5) that transcends the selfless acts of Max and Furiosa.

While *Fury Road* has received the most attention for its gendered representation and post-feminist politics, a critique of toxic masculinity has been a constant undercurrent in the *Mad Max* series since 1979. Johnny the Boy is in some ways, typologically, an early iteration of Nux. He is boyish and likeable yet spends most of the film trying to prove himself to his gang leader Toecutter. In his search to find acceptance amongst his marauding gang he becomes a rapist and murderer and is finally blown to pieces by Max. Similarly, the War Boys and War Pups in *Fury Road* embrace the violent masculinity engendered by Immortan Joe through the cult of the V8, yet they are offered liberation by strong female characters—Furiosa, the breeders and the Vuvalini. Whereas Nux finds redemption through his heroic self-sacrifice, Johnny the Boy does not. As a key villain throughout the first *Mad Max* film and nemesis to both Max and Goose, Johnny the Boy is boyishly coded as either cognitively impaired, a psychopath and/or a drug addict. He is infantilised by Toecutter and rejected as a "scag" who will "never learn" by Bubba Zanetti. The breeders also initially reject Nux in the same way, yelling "who killed the world?!" as they thrust him from the moving war rig. In *Mad Max*, during their first encounter, Max describes Johnny the Boy as being "out of his skull". Johnny repeats that line and then he says "oh, this is it … dementis compo". Johnny the Boy is a powerful symbol—Max fears becoming like him—"you know, a terminal crazy".

Conclusion

This chapter employed theories of gender, trauma, disability and the monster to interrogate the representation of disability and trauma across the *Mad Max* films. *Fury Road,* in particular, presents a large number of characters with disability to explore themes related to gender, ability and the damaging impacts of late capitalism under patriarchy. For example, protagonists Furiosa and Max have an amputated arm and post-traumatic stress disorder (PTSD), respectively, while the antagonist Immortan Joe requires a breathing apparatus and has tumours and boils across his entire body which he covers with a moulded Perspex plate. He preserves autocratic control by deluding his army and serfs into thinking he is all powerful. The War Boys function as a cult-like paramilitary with terminal cancers, some of whom are blind, many who are about to die. As such, disability intersects with gender to incite an aesthetic nervousness throughout the *Mad Max* series, and especially *Fury Road.* From the unanswered cry of women in the film, this trauma is implicitly caused by toxic masculinity.

While George Miller often comments that no clear chronology exists across the four *Mad Max* films—"If you put a gun to my head, I'd say [*Fury Road* occurs] after *Thunderdome*, but it's very loose. I can't even work out the chronology of the first, second and third, let alone the fourth thirty years later" (Davis, 2015)—there is a clear progression of gender representation. In 1979, women perform marginal roles in the film. With the exception of Aunt May they do not act, they are acted upon, and exist in the film solely for the emotion and action they elicit from men. During the films made in the 1980s, *The Road Warrior* and *Beyond Thunderdome,* female characters increasingly adopted important roles with leadership positions in rebuilding post-apocalyptic communities. Yet, intriguingly, these women provoke no emotion and very limited action from Max.

In contrast, *Fury Road* is often celebrated for embracing a strong feminist political agenda. Furiosa's amputated arm performs an integral role in establishing a leadership style in stark contrast to the damaging effects of toxic masculinity. Furiosa is both with and without her prosthesis at key moments in the film to reinforce post-feminist notions of fairness, equality and diversity. At the same time, several male disabled characters populate the world of *Fury Road* to critique toxic masculinity and the demands of patriarchy on young men. In Miller's quartet of action films the preservation of masculinist power and ableism are revealed to be dangerously illusory in imagining the social order to come.

References

Baxter, J. (2017, July 30). How *Mad Max* trained its actors for the apocalypse. Retrieved from http://www.cinemablend.com/new/How-Mad-Max-Trained-Its-Actors-Apocalypse-71285.html

Berger, J. (2004). Trauma without disability, disability without trauma: A disciplinary divide. *JAC, 24*(3), 563–582.

Clarey, A. (2015, May 11). Why you should not go see *Mad Max: Feminist Road. Return of the Kings.* Retrieved from http://www.returnofkings.com/63036/why-you-should-not-go-see-mad-max-feminist-road

Cohen, J. J. (1996). *Monster theory: Reading culture.* Minneapolis, MI: University of Minnesota Press.

Davis, E. (2015). Interview: Director George Miller answers all your big *Mad Max: Fury Road* questions. Retrieved from https://www.fandango.com/movie-news/interview-director-george-miller-answers-all-your-big-mad-max-fury-road-questions-749278

Du Plooy, B. (2018). 'Hope is a mistake, if you can't fix what's broken you go insane': A reading of gender, (s)heroism and redemption in *Mad Max: Fury Road*. *Journal of Gender Studies*, 1–21. https://doi.org/10.1080/09589236.2018.1491395

Elliott, K. (2016). Caring masculinities: Theorizing an emerging concept. *Men and Masculinities, 19*(3), 240–259. https://doi.org/10.1177/1097184X15576203

Enker, D. (1994). Australia and the Australians. In S. Murray (Ed.), *Australian cinema*. St Leonards, NSW: Allen and Unwin.

Frank, A. (1995). *The wounded storyteller: Body, illness and ethics*. Chicago, IL: The University of Chicago Press.

Garland-Thomson, R. (1996). *Freakery: Cultural spectacles of the extraordinary body*. New York, NY: New York University Press.

Garland-Thomson, R. (1997). *Extraordinary bodies: Figuring physical disability in American culture and literature*. New York, NY: Columbia University Press.

Gumb, L. (2018). Trauma and recovery: Finding the ordinary hero in fictional recovery narratives. *Journal of Humanistic Psychology, 58*(4), 460–474.

Haraway, D. (1990). A manifesto for cyborgs: Science, technology, and socialist feminism in the 1980s. In L. J. Nicholson (Ed.), *Feminism/Postmodernism*. New York, NY: Routledge.

Heller-Nicholas, A. (2012). The dark side of mateship: Rape and silence in black-rock. *Screen Education, 68*, 109–114.

Hughes, B. (2009). Wounded/monstrous/abject: A critique of the disabled body in the sociological imaginary. *Disability & Society, 24*(4), 399–410. https://doi.org/10.1080/09687590902876144

Kafer, A. (2013). *Feminist, queer, crip*. Bloomington, IN: Indiana University Press.

Lada-Richards, I. (1998). Foul monster or good saviour? Reflections on ritual monsters. In C. Atherton (Ed.), *Monsters and monstrosity in Greek and Roman culture* (pp. 41–82). Bari, Italy: Levante.

MacInnes, P. (2015, October 2). George Miller: 'The last thing I wanted to do was another *Mad Max* movie'. *The Guardian*. Retrieved from https://www.theguardian.com/film/2015/oct/02/george-miller-on-mad-max-fury-road

Mad Max Wiki. (n.d.). War Boys. Retrieved from https://madmax.fandom.com/wiki/War_Boys

Mathews, S. (1984). *35mm dreams*. Melbourne, VIC: Penguin.

Mott, M., & Dillon, M. (2018, October 8). Beloved South Australian entertainer and disability advocate Quentin Kenihan dies, aged 43. *News.com.au*. Retrieved from https://www.news.com.au/national/south-australia/beloved-south-australian-entertainer-and-disability-advocate-quentin-kenihan-dies-aged-43/news-story/9b0eb77cbae1a272d03c80daae24f3a8

Mulvey, L. (1975). Visual pleasure and narrative cinema. *Screen, 16*(3), 6–18.

Neale, S. (1982). Masculinity as spectacle. *Screen, 24*(6), 2–17. https://doi.org/10.1093/screen/24.6.2

O'Regan, T. (2005). *Australian national cinema*. London, UK; New York, NY: Routledge.

Oliver, M. (1978). The misuse of technology: Walking appliances for paraplegics. *Journal of Medical Engineering & Technology, 2*(2), 69–70.

Penny, L. (2015, May 23). *Mad Max* is a feminist playbook for surviving dystopia. *Buzz Feed*. Retrieved from https://www.buzzfeednews.com/article/laurie-penny/the-fast-and-the-feminist

Sharf, Z. (2018). *Mad Max: Fury Road*: George Miller looks back at filming Charlize Theron's iconic scream in one take. Retrieved from https://www.indiewire.com/2018/04/george-miller-mad-max-fury-road-desert-shot-charlize-theron-scream-1201949892/

Shaw-Williams, H. (2015, May 12). *Mad Max: Fury Road* consultant Eve Ensler calls it a 'Feminist Action Film'. *Screen Rant*. Retrieved from http://screen-rant.com/mad-max-fury-road-eve-ensler-feminism/

Shildrick, M. (2002). *Embodying the monster: Encounters with the vulnerable self.* London, UK: SAGE.

Siebers, T. (2008). *Disability theory*. Ann Arbor, MI: University of Michigan Press.

Siebers, T. (2010). *Disability aesthetics*. Ann Arbor, MI: University of Michigan Press.

Smith, A. (2012). *Hideous progeny: Disability, eugenics, and classic horror cinema*. West Sussex, UK: Columbia University Press.

Times Staff Writer. (1985, July 1). Reagan gets idea from *Rambo* for next time. *LA Times*. Retrieved from http://articles.latimes.com/1985-07-01/news/mn-10009_1_hostage-crisis

Valenti, J. (2015, May 27). Sexists are scared of *Mad Max* because it is a call to dismantle patriarchies. *The Guardian*. Retrieved from https://www.theguardian.com/commentisfree/2015/may/27/sexists-are-scared-of-mad-max-because-it-is-a-call-to-dismantle-patriarchies

Watercutter, A. (2015, May 14). *Mad Max: Fury Road* was worth waiting 30 years for. *Wired*. Retrieved from https://www.wired.com/2015/05/mad-max-fury-road-review/

Wendell, S. (1989). Toward a feminist theory of disability. *Hypatia, 4*(2), 104–124. https://doi.org/10.1111/j.1527-2001.1989.tb00576.x

Wright, A. (2013). *Monstrosity: The human monster in visual culture*. London, UK: I.B. Tauris.

CHAPTER 5

Mythology

Abstract When Tina Turner sang *We Don't Need Another Hero* over the end credits of *Mad Max: Beyond Thunderdome* (1985), it seemed that the trilogy had exhausted its heroic narrative trajectory. However, based on myth scholar Joseph Campbell's works, writer-director-producer George Miller understood that Max's journey remained incomplete and lacked resolution. This chapter therefore considers the cultural and cinematic myths of heroism, trauma and disability alongside Max's character transformation and questions of pre-determinism and fate. It examines the influence of Campbell's "monomyth" across the four films spanning three decades in order to reflect shifting international geopolitics—including petrochemical dependence and globalisation—sociocultural contexts and, significantly, the spectres of Indigenous genocide, all resonating within our emergent epoch now widely understood as the Anthropocene.

Keywords Mythology • Hero • Monomyth • Joseph Campbell • Anthropocene

Myths are frequently construed as inherited, organising and sometimes poetic narratives that explain social function and the conduct of individuals within the world (Rosenberg, 1986). Myths provide insight into human action and often work through intuition, appealing directly to the unconscious (Cotterall, 1979). They are populated by a plethora of gods, the

M. Broderick, K. Ellis, *Trauma and Disability in Mad Max*,
https://doi.org/10.1007/978-3-030-19439-0_5

semi-divine, the superhuman and mundane mortals who transcend their ordinariness to attain the status of heroes. As Rosenberg notes:

> The heroic myths and epics of a society teach its members the appropriate attitudes, behavior, and values of that culture [...] in these myths we see ourselves, drawn larger and grander than we are, yet with our human weaknesses as well as our strengths. (1986, p. xvi)

By undertaking great deeds and inspiring others to follow their example, these heroes become models for their society, garner widespread and long-lasting fame and achieve a type of narrative immortality normally only the preserve of the gods. Myths are usually bound to the (a)historic or prehistoric time of the ancients or to a temporally non-defined spirit realm, or operate within and outside boundaries of normal human perception and interaction. However, in the contemporary sense, modern mythology adapts tales of historical figures into legends and heroes by applying "archetypal forms of myth" (Cotterall, 1979, p. 12). These figures populate the mass media and have tremendous cross-cultural appeal, evident in the post-millennial superhero franchises of the comic-into-movie media of Marvel and DC products.

Mythology, Disability and Trauma

As means to inspire and regulate society, mythological narratives are also informative about trauma and disability. Ancient tales and epics are replete with characters who are impaired and/or traumatised by their experiences, often while on heroic quests, battles or journeys. There are numerous examples amongst archaic texts and lore, with some dating back several millennia, including ancient Mesopotamia and Egypt, the Graeco-Roman empires, Norse, Celtic and Vedic legends and pre-Colombian mythologies. Amongst the deities and heroes—as well as tyrants and monsters—are several characters with externally or self-imposed physical afflictions, inherited disabilities or mental illness. Most common are lameness, blindness, deafness, mutism and speech impediments. Others are born "deformed" or lose limbs in battle or by punishment from the gods. In some cases, a prosthesis is fashioned to aid mobility or dexterity that has become an iconic element of the hero/god's identity. For example, the Indian warrior queen Vishpala lost a leg in battle which was replaced with an iron prosthesis to enable her return to the fight (Szczepanski, 2018). In an epic Creation conflict, the Aztec god Tezcatlipoca severed his right foot which was artificially replaced with black volcanic glass and fused with bone (Cartwright, 2013). The legendary Celtic king Nuada had his sword-wielding right arm cleaved away, later to be substituted with a full-length silver arm/hand (Roric, 2015). Classical Greek myth also abounds with narrative imagery of disfigurement, deformity and disability (Kelley, 2007). Yet, as Martha L. Rose notes, our contemporary sense of ancient Greek physicality is infused with more recent Renaissance and Neoclassical renderings of an idealised, if not perfect, human form:

> In fact, the ancient Greek world was inhabited by people with a wide range of disabilities. In any given public gathering place, one would have seen a much greater variety of physical conditions than one would see in the developed world today. (Rose, 2006, p. 9)

Indeed, despite recorded taunting and mistreatment, the Greeks did not categorise people based on perceived physical disability, neither were they wholly prevented from undertaking certain roles nor excluded from society and shunted away into special areas.

Similarly, earlier Sumerian creation myths informed Mesopotamian society in surprisingly tolerant ways (Walls, 2007, p. 18), where those with disabilities—for example, the maimed, blind, paralysed, cognitively impaired, incontinent, barren and sexless—were provided "a social position and productive economic role" by the gods such as musician, silversmith, courtier, weaver, priestess and administrator. According to Walls, rather than these ancient myths "naming 'disability' as a means to exclude some persons from city life", they recognise their "otherness", with each becoming a functioning member within the social organisation where many are given "technical skills and high social status consistent with their abilities" (2007, p. 19).

One of the archetypal characters of ancient mythology is Oedipus (meaning "swollen footed", a deformity imposed by his father), who walks with a limp and, later, is traumatised by the pre-destined—though inadvertent—murder of his father and marrying of his mother. He plucks out his eyes in despair and self-retribution, adding blindness to his lameness. A renowned, cautionary tale spanning millennia, the Oedipal legend became a foundation of twentieth century Freudian psychoanalysis—the "nuclear complex" of human neuroses (Freud, 1960; Levin, 1948). After defeating the monstrous Sphinx, Oedipus, the limping hero and liberator of Thebes, is condemned to wander the wilderness following the shocking revelation and self-realisation of his acts. Hence, despite his heroic deeds, Oedipus is made doubly tragic. His impairments result from deliberate attempts to circumvent prophecy, firstly by his father's maiming of his feet and his—unsuccessful—infanticide by exposure/abandonment (Corbier, 2001) and, secondly, by Oedipus fleeing Corinth to avoid the same fate foretold by the Oracle at Delphi, yet still he brings about the events and subsequently blinds himself. Unlike many Greek and Roman myths regarding other disabilities, those rendered blind are often compensated by divine intervention, enabling these victims the power of prophecy, clairvoyance or magic (Kelley, 2007). However, in the case of Oedipus, there is no customary magical compensation by the gods for either his paternal injury (lameness) or his self-imposed disability (blindness).

Miller and Mythology

As we have argued in Chap. 3, contested issues surrounding the representation of "able-bodiedness" or "sound-mindedness" inform readings of the *Mad Max* quartet, much of which are drawn from some of the aforementioned, pre-existing medical and social concepts of disability. For example, during the pre-production phase of *Beyond Thunderdome*, circa 1983, George Miller recounted that he understood, in retrospect, while working on *Mad Max* he had become "the unwitting servant" of the "collective unconscious" and, having been "made aware of the workings of mythology", he was "in wonder of it" (Mathews, 1984, p. 34). As Miller's comment acknowledges, prior to *Fury Road* both *The Road Warrior* and *Beyond Thunderdome* had consciously drawn from and applied narrative logics based on the works of myth scholar Joseph Campbell. This chapter considers how *Fury Road* has contributed to, or at times usurped, Campbell's cyclical journey of the monomythic hero.

In his influential work, *The Hero with a Thousand Faces,* Campbell's defines the monomyth as:

> The standard path of the mythological adventure of the hero is a magnification of the formula represented in the rites of passage: *separation-initiation-return*. (1973, p. 30)

The *Mad Max* quartet follows this path by foregrounding the evolution of Max as a hero—from his rejection of the "outside world" due to personal

films have influenced world cinema and popular culture as widely as George Miller's *Mad Max* movies" (Martin, 2003, p. 1). Paradoxically, given the era's "end of history" rhetoric, the most significant and dominant generic movement of this period was the (re)emergence of "the Post-apocalyptic Hero as an Exterminating Angel", a subgenre that championed the survivors' heroic acts of justice, reprisal and/or vengeance (Broderick, 1993; Cumbow, 1984; Newman, 1999). Mostly set after a nuclear war, what little fabric of community that remains is constantly threatened by rampaging bands of marauders, challenged only by a (self)righteous individual and occasionally by smaller, organised groups.

Prophecy and Pre-determinism

In both Jewish and Christian theology, the prophecy anticipating an apocalyptic hero-saviour was a means by which to spiritually and psychologically overcome the immediate calamity of social persecution. This was further tempered by scriptural revelations forecasting an end to the era of oppression via the millennial intervention of a warrior-hero, and with it oblivion and eternal damnation of his foes (Cohn, 1970). This notion of myth-making through storytelling and cultural transmission was also important to Miller in making the *Mad Max* movies. The filmmaker maintains he was:

> attracted to the notion of using a narrator for *The Road Warrior* because it said very clearly that this is *storytelling, fable, mythology*. It also served to move the film yet another degree into another time [...] into a mythological framework. (Miller as cited in Peary, 1984, p. 280)

For example, *The Road Warrior* features both a narrated prologue and epilogue. This narration explicitly establishes a global apocalyptic battle between superpowers, one that is sparked by entropy and decadence. Structurally, within the film's unfolding narrative, the prologue establishes the history of Max and the context of society's "fall" *retrospectively:* "Two mighty warrior tribes" started a war over the fight for oil that "engulfed them all". The events and Max's heroic exploits are further relayed in closing, as a narrated *flashback*, one that propels the oral mythologising temporally into a distant future. The narrated coda comes as a literal revelation, something outside/beyond diegetic time which momentarily unsettles identification and corrupts the linear-narrative perspective, although, sig-

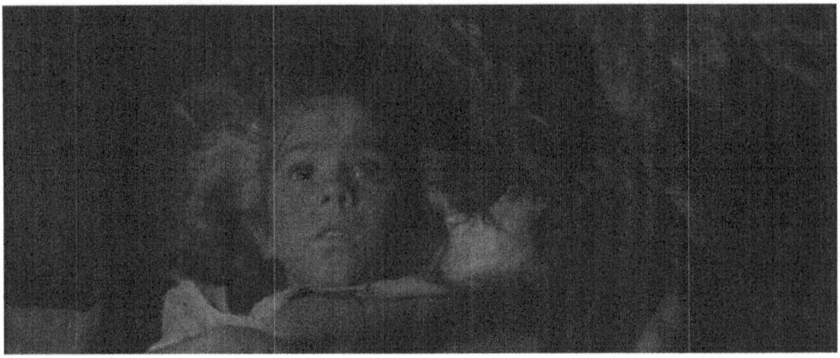

Fig. 5.1 The Feral Kid (Emil Minty) in *The Road Warrior*. Like Paul Klee and Walter Benjamin's *Angel of History*, he looks back from a future-present to narrate the future as past

nificantly, the film does not privilege the spectator with an image of the boomerang-wielding Feral Kid, now the Great Northern Tribe leader, only a craggy voice and the narrator's self-avowal. This retelling affirms the tone of messianic pre-determinism and fate operating within the plot by enclosing Max's monomythic hero adventures not as linear events unfolding at random nor as cause and effect throughout the film's duration, but as *past* events, now related from an omniscient and epic vantage (Fig. 5.1).

Similarly, *Beyond Thunderdome* privileges a significant tale of origin—the Lost Tribe of children who rescue Max from the desert wilderness after his exile from Bartertown. Theirs is a mythic tale of origin *and* (pre) destiny. The narrated oral epic—the ritualised "tell"—employs a type of poetic, pidgin discourse to evoke the apocalyptic events of atomic warfare, contamination, nuclear winter, mass death and survival. Hence, this sequence corresponds directly with the return of the hero-messiah foretold in—and given spiritually agency by—the act of (re)telling. It also demonstrates Campbell's view of the monomyth and its extension into action (Fig. 5.2):

> Myths are the mental supports of rites; rites, the physical enactment of myths. By absorbing the myths of his social group and participating in rites, the youngster is structured to accord with his social as well as natural environment, and turned from an amorphous nature product, prematurely

Fig. 5.2 The Tell, a Panavision-shaped ceremonial frame by which the Lost Tribe record and remember past events and prophecy, including the messianic return of Captain Walker, whom they identify as Max

> born, into a defined and competent member of some specific, efficiently functioning social order. (Campbell, 1973, p. 35)

Film historian Will Wright has also argued that the hero, while intent on vengeance, is at some point confronted by a member of society who points out his individualistic, antisocial behaviour (1975, p. 158). For Campbell, the hero must ultimately not be outside the range of communal empathy:

> The myths of failure touch us with the tragedy of life, but those of success only with their own incredibility. And yet, if the monomyth is to fulfil its promise, not human failure or superhuman success but *human success* is what we have to be shown. (1973, pp. 206–207)

By his initial abandonment of society at the end of *Mad Max* and refusal of what Campbell describes as "the call"—in which Max initially rejects his Captain's desire to give society back its "heroes"—true to the monomyth, the first encounter of the hero's journey is with a "protective figure", such as *The Road Warrior's* Feral Kid and the "trickster" Gyro Captain, who "tests" Max's mind, reflexes and body. The snake-wielding Gyro Captain's role becomes even more problematic in *Beyond Thunderdome*, from "trickster" to "journeyman to the afterworld" of post-nuked Sydney. The Lost Tribe of feral children connotes salvation, and recuperation for Max and, like the descendants of the ten lost tribes of Israel, as Norman Cohn notes, they survive in hidden places, unknown to the rest of the world (Cohn, 1970, p. 12). What such figures represent mythologically, according to Joseph Campbell, are the "benign, protecting power of destiny", all of which problematically advances the inevitability of a pre-determined future.

This persistent fatalistic reading, indeed celebration, by Campbell raises questions about his advocacy of an unseen, relentless and pre-ordained cosmic scheme that exerts force onto unwitting players. However, the absence of any real self-determining space afforded the hero in Campbell's theory is troubling, if not reactionary. Collective order, consensus and community institutions are irrelevant. Campbell's rhetoric relishing the hero's individuality and rejection of the social, unquestioningly impelling us following one's destiny ("bliss"), where might equals right is, borders on engendering protofascist ideology.

Nevertheless, quite often in mythology, the journey-quest of the hero leads to social inertia rather than rebirth, with the hero failing to pass on his knowledge or skills to the community. Campbell argues:

> the norm of the monomyth, requires that the hero shall now begin the labor of bringing the runes of wisdom [...] back into the kingdom of humanity, where the boon may redound to the renewing of the community, the nation, the world [...] But the responsibility has frequently been refused. (1973, p. 193)

Such a trope of refusing to pass on to the world his experience is evident in the nihilistic act of revenge closing the first film, and in Max's "fulfilled contract" rejection of any assistance for the besieged community in *The Road Warrior,* acts which portray him simply retreating further into an alienated and self-destructive sense of autonomy. However, in keeping with his messianic hero construction, Max's role in the first two films is best outlined by Campbell where the mythological hero is the champion not of things become, but of things *becoming*. He is both an unwitting and unwilling agent of end-time transition:

> the dragon to be slain by him is precisely the monster of the status quo: Holdfast, the keeper of the past [...] The tyrant is proud, and therein lies his [sic] doom. (Campbell, 1973, p. 334)

Such adversarial "proud tyrants" who conform with Campbell's monomythic definition are personified by a number of characters, including

na and psycho-social symptoms of PTSD. Despite these limi-
is propensity for manic aggression (as discussed in Chap. 2),
ally demonstrates a capacity to move beyond narcissistic
d self-preservation at all costs to work collectively for com-
it in order to ensure a more egalitarian future, a future in
l most likely never participate and remain at the margins.

Conclusion

further into the twenty-first century, films entertaining global
m nuclear Armageddon to catastrophic climate events—per-
cular commercial products, entertaining billions. The interna-
ffice and critical success that has followed *Fury Road* will likely
ontinuance of the franchise's narrative mythology for years to
oubtedly set amidst a radioactive, resource-depleted and
ilderness, as a "future anterior", a what "will have been"
2011, p. 25), one richly imagined, mythologically, as both
testament to the Anthropocene.

References

. (1993). Surviving Armageddon: Beyond the imagination of disas-
Fiction Studies, 20(3), 362–382.
. (2015). Apocalypse Australis: eschatology on southern screens.
rts, 608–620. https://doi.org/10.1080/02560046.2015.1125091
L. (2017). *Miller and Max: George Miller and the making of a film*
ndon, UK: Hardy Grant.
). (1995). *Apocalypse theory and the ends of the world*. Oxford, UK:

(1973). *The hero with a thousand faces*. Princeton, NJ: Princeton
Press.
M. (2013, August 14). Tezcatlipoca. *Ancient History Encyclopedia*.
from https://www.ancient.eu/Tezcatlipoca/
70). *The pursuit of the millennium: Revolutionary millenarians and*
narchists of the Middle Ages. Oxford, UK: Oxford University Press.
(2001). Child exposure and abandonment. In S. Dixon (Ed.),
class and kin in the Roman world (pp. 52–73). London, UK:

(1979). *A dictionary of world mythology*. London, UK: Book Club

Nightrider in *Mad Max* (who loses his life after failing at "chicken of the road") and Bubba Zanetti who over-confidently drops his guard when he fells Max: "I know what I'm doing", he tells Toecutter. Others include Humungus and his marauders in *The Road Warrior* who represent the decaying and entropic remnants of a moribund society and, of course, both Aunty Entity in *Beyond Thunderdome*, whose complacent dominion is usurped by an Underworld rebellion, and Immortan Joe, whose hubris and blind ambition leads to defeat in *Fury Road*.

As a trickster-hero, Max the pursued becomes the pursuer of Toecutter's gang and the Humungus who is fooled into following the wrong group of vehicles. Similarly, Max miraculously returns from Gulag to destroy Bartertown and liberate his allies. Ultimately, the status of Max as a redemptive, mythological hero is confirmed by the act of him being the unwitting decoy of the Humungus in *The Road Warrior*, and then as a *deliberate* decoy-sacrifice who enables the Lost Tribe to escape from Aunty Entity in *Beyond Thunderdome*. In the atemporal rebooting of *Fury Road*, Max's winning strategy is to abandon self-interest, turn around Furiosa's group of escapee women and return them to liberate Immortan Joe's despotic, desert citadel. For writer-director George Miller, again echoing Campbell, such conscious intercessions demonstrate "when Max begins to be, in the classic sense, heroic" (Mathews, 1984, p. 251). Each are catalytic interventions permitting rebirth of their communal microcosms, whether this be via the safe passage of petroleum reserves in *The Road Warrior*, or enabling a chosen elect of youth to escape the desert and repopulate Sydney in *Beyond Thunderdome*, or unleashing quarantined water supplies back into a survivor community in *Fury Road*. As such, the *Mad Max* series conforms to the monomythic narrative trope of the hero's journey and quest. As Campbell asserts, "The effect of the successful adventure of the hero is the unlocking and release again of the flow of life into the body of the world" (1973, p. 40).

These selfless acts by Max in *Beyond Thunderdome* and *Fury Road* herald not only rebirth for the hero, but for the entire world—a return of Campbell's cosmogenic cycle. However, as in Judeo-Christian theology, the willing sacrifice of the individual for the group means Max is unable or unwilling to immediately partake of its fruits (Mathews, 1984, p. 259). In opposition to the *ironic* hero deed in *The Road Warrior* of driving the decoy tanker—which permits the escape and establishment of a future tribe ruled by the Feral Kid, narratively related via an unexpected mythopoeic oral epilogue—Max's acts of near-apotheosis which closes the third film

Fig. 5.3 With the defeat of Immortan Joe, the previously held captive group of lactating mothers prepare to release the vast reserves of sequestered water for the masses congregating below the elevated Citadel

and penultimately concludes *Fury Road*, are reified for the audience by witnessing their liberating and rejuvenating results. Examples of this include Savannah Nix's oral history, now a New World mother nursing an infant before the tribe in the repopulated skeletal remains of Sydney, and Furiosa and the women elders entering the citadel as the lactating mothers unleashing Immortan Joe's previously rationed reservoir of water (Fig. 5.3).

The further role and adventure of the monomythic hero, Campbell maintains, is to bring his world-shattering knowledge to the rest of civilisation. Max's journeys are therefore incomplete since, as Campbell reminds us, like many classical heroes: "The hero of yesterday becomes the tyrant of tomorrow, unless he crucifies himself today" (1973, p. 353). To complete the monomythic cycle and apocalyptic prophecy, Max, as Messiah, must be either victorious in one last battle against the allegorical Antichrist and usher in the millennium—or some form of transcendental Rapture for the elect, as depicted in the literal ascensions at the end of both *Beyond Thunderdome* and *Fury Road*—or the hero is feted and ultimately assumes the tragic figure of tyrant, himself becoming another's Antichrist, destined to be usurped and slain.

The failure of Max throughout all four films, in Campbell's terms, to return to the civilised world, is one faced by most monomythic protagonists:

> The first problem of the returning h
> ence of the soul-satisfying vision of fu
> banalities and noisy obscenities of life
> easy thing is to commit the whole co
> (1973, p. 218)

It is clear that George Miller's new
serves the outright rejection of any s
Furiosa at the film's conclusion, Ton
the ragtag throng assembled at the f
Max silently makes his choice, prefe
wasteland, literally turning his back
While *Fury Road* perpetuates the
tional, future post-holocaust domair
temporally frozen by the impasse
universe, this fourth *Mad Max* film,
for 30 years, could have been one t
hero trajectory. This might have beer
cosmogenic cycle, with Max played
slated for the film), who either retur
over or rebuilds Bartertown, becom
Immortan Joe, becomes the ageing,
out of the wilderness, approaching fr
hero appears, vaguely familiar, possib
and skill ensues, and ultimately the
Max in the final scene, freeing the c
killed? Why, by the unnamed strange
Yet at the conclusion of the fou
rebooted Max out in the wilderness.
to refine, distil and purify the heroic
mous character, now an ageless cypl
atemporal, post-cataclysmic realm. I
teleology, Max is destined to wander
the contemporary zeitgeist, simultane
the concerns of global audiences facir
nationalism and anthropogenic clim
from now" as the entropic first *Mad*
nuclear skirmish" and other toxic leg
"Killed the World", Max has borne

physical trau
tations and
Max contin
avoidance a
munal bene
which he wi

As we move
disaster—fr
sist as specta
tional box o
propel the c
come, und
despoiled w
(Rosenthal,
witness and

Broderick, M
ter. *Scienc*
Broderick, M
Critical A
Buckmaster,
legend. L
Bull, M. (Ed
Blackwell.
Campbell, J.
University
Cartwright,
Retrieved
Cohn, N. (1
mystical a
Corbier, M.
Childhood
Routledg
Cotterall, A.
Associate

Fig. 5.3 With the defeat of Immortan Joe, the previously held captive group of lactating mothers prepare to release the vast reserves of sequestered water for the masses congregating below the elevated Citadel

and penultimately concludes *Fury Road*, are reified for the audience by witnessing their liberating and rejuvenating results. Examples of this include Savannah Nix's oral history, now a New World mother nursing an infant before the tribe in the repopulated skeletal remains of Sydney, and Furiosa and the women elders entering the citadel as the lactating mothers unleashing Immortan Joe's previously rationed reservoir of water (Fig. 5.3).

The further role and adventure of the monomythic hero, Campbell maintains, is to bring his world-shattering knowledge to the rest of civilisation. Max's journeys are therefore incomplete since, as Campbell reminds us, like many classical heroes: "The hero of yesterday becomes the tyrant of tomorrow, unless he crucifies himself today" (1973, p. 353). To complete the monomythic cycle and apocalyptic prophecy, Max, as Messiah, must be either victorious in one last battle against the allegorical Antichrist and usher in the millennium—or some form of transcendental Rapture for the elect, as depicted in the literal ascensions at the end of both *Beyond Thunderdome* and *Fury Road*—or the hero is feted and ultimately assumes the tragic figure of tyrant, himself becoming another's Antichrist, destined to be usurped and slain.

The failure of Max throughout all four films, in Campbell's terms, to return to the civilised world, is one faced by most monomythic protagonists:

Nightrider in *Mad Max* (who loses his life after failing at "chicken of the road") and Bubba Zanetti who over-confidently drops his guard when he fells Max: "I know what I'm doing", he tells Toecutter. Others include Humungus and his marauders in *The Road Warrior* who represent the decaying and entropic remnants of a moribund society and, of course, both Aunty Entity in *Beyond Thunderdome*, whose complacent dominion is usurped by an Underworld rebellion, and Immortan Joe, whose hubris and blind ambition leads to defeat in *Fury Road*.

As a trickster-hero, Max the pursued becomes the pursuer of Toecutter's gang and the Humungus who is fooled into following the wrong group of vehicles. Similarly, Max miraculously returns from Gulag to destroy Bartertown and liberate his allies. Ultimately, the status of Max as a redemptive, mythological hero is confirmed by the act of him being the unwitting decoy of the Humungus in *The Road Warrior*, and then as a *deliberate* decoy-sacrifice who enables the Lost Tribe to escape from Aunty Entity in *Beyond Thunderdome*. In the atemporal rebooting of *Fury Road*, Max's winning strategy is to abandon self-interest, turn around Furiosa's group of escapee women and return them to liberate Immortan Joe's despotic, desert citadel. For writer-director George Miller, again echoing Campbell, such conscious intercessions demonstrate "when Max begins to be, in the classic sense, heroic" (Mathews, 1984, p. 251). Each are catalytic interventions permitting rebirth of their communal microcosms, whether this be via the safe passage of petroleum reserves in *The Road Warrior*, or enabling a chosen elect of youth to escape the desert and repopulate Sydney in *Beyond Thunderdome*, or unleashing quarantined water supplies back into a survivor community in *Fury Road*. As such, the *Mad Max* series conforms to the monomythic narrative trope of the hero's journey and quest. As Campbell asserts, "The effect of the successful adventure of the hero is the unlocking and release again of the flow of life into the body of the world" (1973, p. 40).

These selfless acts by Max in *Beyond Thunderdome* and *Fury Road* herald not only rebirth for the hero, but for the entire world—a return of Campbell's cosmogenic cycle. However, as in Judeo-Christian theology, the willing sacrifice of the individual for the group means Max is unable or unwilling to immediately partake of its fruits (Mathews, 1984, p. 259). In opposition to the *ironic* hero deed in *The Road Warrior* of driving the decoy tanker—which permits the escape and establishment of a future tribe ruled by the Feral Kid, narratively related via an unexpected mythopoeic oral epilogue—Max's acts of near-apotheosis which closes the third film

> The first problem of the returning he
> ence of the soul-satisfying vision of fu
> banalities and noisy obscenities of life.
> easy thing is to commit the whole coı
> (1973, p. 218)

It is clear that George Miller's newe
serves the outright rejection of any su
Furiosa at the film's conclusion, Tom
the ragtag throng assembled at the fo
Max silently makes his choice, prefer
wasteland, literally turning his back o

While *Fury Road* perpetuates the
tional, future post-holocaust domain,
temporally frozen by the impasse o
universe, this fourth *Mad Max* film, s
for 30 years, could have been one th
hero trajectory. This might have been
cosmogenic cycle, with Max played b
slated for the film), who either returı
over or rebuilds Bartertown, becomiı
Immortan Joe, becomes the ageing, c
out of the wilderness, approaching fro
hero appears, vaguely familiar, possibl
and skill ensues, and ultimately the s
Max in the final scene, freeing the ca
killed? Why, by the unnamed stranger'

Yet at the conclusion of the four
rebooted Max out in the wilderness. Iı
to refine, distil and purify the heroic ı
mous character, now an ageless cyph
atemporal, post-cataclysmic realm. D
teleology, Max is destined to wander t
the contemporary zeitgeist, simultaneo
the concerns of global audiences facinş
nationalism and anthropogenic clima
from now" as the entropic first *Mad M*
nuclear skirmish" and other toxic lega
"Killed the World", Max has borne t

physical trauday after doomsday. In D. Peary (Ed.),
tations and lpp. 35–42). New York, NY: Dolphin.
Max contin *apocalypse: Theory and cultural practice*
avoidance arnia: University Press.
munal bene*blances between the psychic lives of savages*
which he wi
and literature. San Diego, CA: Harvest.
n Babel: The postmodernist controversy.
Press.
ity in Greece and Rome. In H. Avalos,
As we move*his abled body: Rethinking disabilities in*
disaster—frA: Society of Biblical Literature.
sist as specta*lex: The secret history of comic book heroes.*
tional box o
propel the c in history and psychiatry. *Psychiatry,*
come, und
despoiled wSydney, NSW: Currency Press.
(Rosenthal, ourne, VIC: Penguin.
witness and Retrieved from https://www.youtube.
les of survival and Crocodile Dundee.
End of the world cinema. London, UK:

Broderick, M
ter. *Scien*gh Court and surveyors. *The Australian*
Broderick, M from http://www.csdila.unimelb.edu.
*Critical A*e/artic7.htm
Buckmaster, d *The Road Warrior:* An interview with
legend. L*OMNI's screen flights/screen fantasies*
Bull, M. (Edn.
Blackwellamous sword of light. Retrieved from
Campbell, Jmyths-legends/king-nuada-and-his-
Universit
Cartwright, *us: Transforming disability in Ancient*
Retrievedhigan Press.
Cohn, N. (1 *An anthology of great myths and epics.*
mystical
Corbier, M*sm: Literature, catastrophe, and the poli-*
*Childhoo*ham University Press.
Routledgarrior women of Asia. Retrieved from
Cotterall, Ary-warrior-women-of-asia-195819
Associate

Walls, N. H. (2007). The origins of the disabled body: Disability in ancient Mesopotamia. In H. Avalos, S. J. Melcher, & J. Schipper (Eds.), *This abled body: Rethinking disabilities in biblical studies* (pp. 13–30). Atlanta, GA: Society of Biblical Literature.

White, G. (2008). The bush tucker survival guide: Survival, tracking and awareness – The ancient skills for living with the earth. Retrieved from http://www.survival.org.au/bush_tucker_survival_guide.php

Williams, P. (2005). Beyond *Mad Max* III: Race, empire, and heroism on post-apocalyptic terrain. *Science Fiction Studies, 32*(2), 301–315.

Williams, P. (2011). *Race, ethnicity and nuclear war: Representations of nuclear weapons and post-apocalyptic worlds. Liverpool.* UK: Liverpool University Press.

Winterbach, H. (2006). Heroes and superheroes: From myth to the American comic book. *South African Journal of Art History, I*(1), 114–134.

Wright, W. (1975). *Sixguns & society: A structural study of the Western*. Berkeley, CA: University of California Press.

CHAPTER 6

Fandom and Beyond

Abstract Mad Max is an open-ended character upon which audiences have placed their own meanings. In this chapter, we conclude the book by considering the role of fandom in the longevity of the series, from queer readings and critiques, to Mad Max museums and fan gatherings in Australia, the USA and Japan, to several tumblr pages dedicated to the representation of disability and trauma within *Fury Road*. It is through these sites that the intersections between disability and trauma in *Fury Road*, and by extension the preceding films, are most clearly articulated. While the *Mad Max* films are recognised for depicting trauma, the representation of disability has received far less attention. Yet as we have demonstrated throughout this book, the disabled body is the primary tool through which Miller is able to make his most powerful, though subtle, cultural critiques.

Keywords Mad Max • Fandom • Disability • Trauma

In an interview published on the movie ticket website Fandango, George Miller describes the origins of the Doof Warrior, one of the more popular peripheral characters in *Mad Max: Fury Road*:

> For me, it was all about how someone who is blind survives in this place. How does someone weak survive the apocalypse? He survived because he

M. Broderick, K. Ellis, *Trauma and Disability in Mad Max*,
https://doi.org/10.1007/978-3-030-19439-0_6

> was blind—because he lived deep in an unlit mine, where it was an advantage to be blind. (Miller, as cited in Davis, 2015)

Miller's assertion that the Doof Warrior survived *because* he is blind offers a critique of what we have referred throughout this book as the ideology of ability. Whereas people with disability are typically represented as being at a disadvantage, or as less than human, in popular cinema representation, Miller positions the Doof Warrior's blindness as a strength.

The filmmaker frequently takes this critical approach to disability throughout the series. As discussed throughout this book, several visibly disabled characters populate the *Mad Max* quartet, yet they are never represented as being at a disadvantage or as being less than human. Like the Doof Warrior's ability to survive in total darkness as described in Miller's backstory, disabled characters in *Mad Max* often have a highly specialised capacity that is crucial to a post-apocalyptic world. Further, while disability is common throughout *Mad Max*, characters' impairments are rarely mentioned. This is particularly noticeable as the world descends further into (post-)apocalypse and increasing numbers of impaired bodies populate and attempt to rebuild it. As such, investigating Miller's various references to disability in the context of his four *Mad Max* films reveals an unexplored dimension to his work as it critiques the ideology of ability and raises questions about the potential intersection between critical disability and critical trauma studies.

Miller's descriptions of the Doof Warrior's origin have elicited passionate responses from the fan community. While many embraced hearing more from Miller as the creator of this character, others, such as Devin Faraci, argued that it took away from the experience of making meaning from the film in the context of individual audience members' experiences:

> if you love *Fury Road* you love every time this insane character shows up onscreen, and you sort of want more of him. But George Miller gives you just enough—you always want to be left slightly wanting with guys like that, the tertiary flavor characters. [...] Going deeper isn't always a good idea. (Faraci, 2015)

Faraci continues:

> I get wanting more—that's the nature of fandom. But sometimes not getting that more is the best thing that can happen to us. [...] Yes, we want to

> know more, but sometimes knowing more leads us to experiencing it less. What had been an exercise in the imagination turns into a rote recital of facts and figures. What had been mythic becomes mundane. (Faraci, 2015)

Indeed, fandom has played an important role in the longevity of the *Mad Max* series, from critiques and queer readings to several tumblr pages dedicated to the representation of disability and trauma, in particular within *Fury Road*. It is through these sites that the intersections between disability and trauma in the franchise's latest offering and, by extension, the preceding films, are most clearly articulated:

> max is, disabled. he is deeply, deeply mentally ill. he has auditory and visual hallucinations and is skirting the edge of non-verbal. when the dag says "i thought you weren't crazy anymore," it's doubly funny because in no universe is he ever not going to be crazy. it's just that with his new family, he has one hell of a support network and is able to be something resembling functional. (nataluna, 2015)

The strong social connections and personal relationships—such as those Max discovered with Furiosa, Nux, the breeders and the Vuvalini—have had a significant impact on the reintegration of people experiencing post-traumatic stress disorder (PTSD) into the community (McFarlane, Hodson, Van Hooff, & Davies, 2011).

We began this book by quoting a 1979 interview with George Miller (Miller, as cited in Beilby & Murray, 1979, p. 369) in which he professed a hope that his first *Mad Max* film would start a "conversation" about (road) trauma. Though Miller acknowledged doubts that any single film could necessarily achieve this, media reception theory confirms that it can and does. While disability representation remains a contentious issue, the conversations that even problematic representations elicit in online forums, or amongst fans, offer an important reimaging of disability through which community can be created (Ellis, 2015).

Throughout this book, we have shown how disability pervades the world of *Mad Max*. In the post-apocalyptic world, disability is commonplace. Yet characters are neither sentimentalised nor isolated because of their impairments. Ideologically, this is a completely different environment for people with disability, as Brent Walter Cline explains:

> Disability is considered a banal reality in this world. Only the audience is horrified by The People Eater's swollen legs and wonders how Furiosa lost